National Geographic
Bee
Official Study Guide

by
Stephen F. Cunha

NATIONAL GEOGRAPHIC

Washington, D.C.

In memory of John Joseph Ferguson and Ann Judge, who perished aboard American Airlines Flight 77, which crashed into the Pentagon on September 11, 2001. They were traveling to California with six Washington, D.C., teachers and students as part of an educational field trip sponsored by the National Geographic Society. Joe and Ann were tireless, visionary supporters of the Society's education outreach programs. Their enduring work directly benefits countless teachers and students throughout North America.—SFC

Copyright © 2002 National Geographic Society; updated 2004
Published by the National Geographic Society. All rights reserved. Reproduction of the whole or any part of the contents without written permission from the National Geographic Society is prohibited.

The text type is set in New Caledonia; headlines are set in Clarendon.

All questions and place-names were accurate and current at the date of their actual use in the National Geographic Bee.

Library of Congress Cataloging-in-Publication Data
Cunha, Stephen F.
  National Geographic Bee official study guide / by Stephen F. Cunha.
    v. cm.
Includes index.
Contents: The why of where: defining geography--Bee basics: understanding the contest--Top ten study tips--Conquering the questions--Tips from bee finalists--Resources Genghis Khan would have loved.
  ISBN 0-7922-7850-X (pbk.)
  1. National Geographic Bee--Juvenile literature.
  2. Geography--Competitions--United States--Juvenile literature. 3. School contests--United States--Juvenile literature. [1. National Geographic Bee.
  2. Geography--Competitions. 3. Contests.] I. Title.
  G74 .C86 2002
  910'.79'73--dc21
                                        2002003423

Printed in the United States of America

Contents

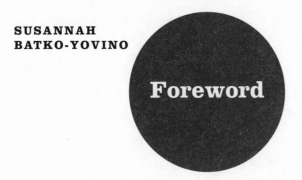

**SUSANNAH
BATKO-YOVINO**

Foreword

Geography was the last thing on my mind on September 11.

Yet, as I watched news coverage of the terrorist attacks in the days and weeks following them, I began to notice the maps. Street maps of downtown New York City, maps of the northeastern United States where the planes had struck, and, later, maps of a remote and dangerous corner of the Earth known as Afghanistan. These maps—more accurately, the political, economic, cultural, and historical geography that these maps depicted— helped answer the most pressing questions: Who were the attackers? Where did they come from? Why did they attack the United States? A thorough knowledge of geography can help us understand all of these issues.

The National Geographic Bee is a great way to learn about geography and the world around us. Each of you will have your own expectations as you prepare to participate. Those of you competing for the first time may be a little scared; those of you entering the Bee for the last time because of age or grade restrictions may be putting quite a bit of pressure on yourselves to do well. But if you think of the Bee not as a contest to be won but as a way to exercise your curiosity and learn more about the world around you, you will succeed even if you don't come out the overall winner.

As you pursue this year's National Geographic Bee Championship, keep in mind that geography is far more than a collection of random facts. Rather, it is one of the best ways to answer the difficult questions posed by our everchanging, complex, and fascinating planet and the people who live on it. Simply by participating in the Bee, you are working to expand your understanding of the world around you—an understanding that I expect will serve you well not only throughout your academic careers but also for the rest of your lives.

Good luck!

Susannah Batko-Yovino
Champion
1990 National Geographic Bee

*I like Geography best,
he said, because your
mountains and rivers
know the secret. Pay no
attention to boundaries.*
—BRIAN ANDREAS,
AMERICAN POET

Introduction

This book will help you prepare for the National Geographic Bee. It is written to answer the most common question that students, teachers, and parents ask of Bee officials: "What's the best way to study for the Bee?" The comprehensive nature of geography makes it hard to offer an easy answer. Most academic contests in spelling and math provide a word or problem list that makes preparation easier. Although you can pinpoint some aspects of the Bee, a good showing requires understanding the nature of geography. In essence, you must learn the fundamental geographic patterns that will help you think geographically. This book presents a framework for learning how to conquer this immense and fascinating subject.

The first chapter explores the world of geography and explains why it is so important to study the subject. Then the origin and purpose of the Bee as well as the structure and format of the contest are discussed. Chapter 3 provides tips on how and what to study for the Bee. Chapter 4 tells you how to look for clues in the questions and use the study tips to come up with the correct answers, then provides lots of real Bee questions so you can test yourself. Bee winners offer advice and inspiration in Chapter 5, and resources that will help you study are evaluated in Chapter 6. The Note to Teachers discusses various initiatives and support groups available for teaching geography more effectively and helping students prepare for the Bee.

Although we live at the dawn of the digital age, Thomas Jefferson's ideal regarding the truly educated person still stands:

> "In the elementary schools will be taught reading, writing, common arithmetic, and general notions of geography. In the district colleges, ancient and modern languages, geography fully, a higher degree of numerical arithmetic...and the elementary principles of navigation."
> —Thomas Jefferson to M. Correa da Serra (1817)

Jefferson believed that a balanced curriculum produced more capable and enlightened citizens than one that focused on just one or two subjects. Although Jefferson never booted up a computer to surf the Web or e-mail his friends, he correctly forecast the value of exercising all parts of the human brain. Were he alive today, he would be pleased by your interest in geography and in the world around you.

What kind of young people enter the Bee? The Society's staff and those of us who work with them have 12 years of data on this very subject. We find that Bee kids play instruments and compete in sports. Many run for student government and join school clubs. Some tour the globe with their parents; others journey mostly in their imaginations. Some kids say their favorite subject is math; others say literature, physical education, or even—gasp—geography. There are tall and short kids, big and small kids, funny kids, and very, very serious kids. Bee kids hail from our largest cities and smallest towns (the first national champion attended a one-room schoolhouse in rural Kansas). Some attend public and private schools; others are homeschooled. What unites them is a natural curiosity about our world.

This book can help you be more competitive at every level of the contest. But advancing through the rounds should not be the only reason to enter the Bee or to study these chapters. The real benefit comes from learning what geography is all about, and that alone will enrich your life forever. You'll be amazed how geography makes you a better reader, a more knowledgeable historian, a better mathematician, and a more versatile scientist. Geography links other subjects into a seamless whole whose sum greatly exceeds its parts. Most important, studying geography will help you become a more sensitive and aware citizen of our global community.

Let the adventure begin!

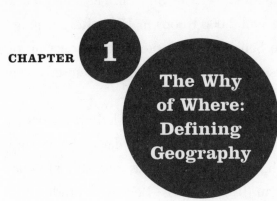

CHAPTER **1**

The Why of Where: Defining Geography

*From space I saw Earth—
indescribably beautiful
with the scars of national
boundaries gone.*
—ASTRONAUT MUHAMMAD
AHMAD FARIS, SYRIA (1988)

Imagine captaining a 17th-century merchant ship with a crew of 200 and a cargo hold stuffed with exotic goods from the Far East. You are London-bound to exchange your booty for gold coins and more shipping contracts from anxious merchants. Gazing across the Indian Ocean at sunrise, you take stock of the possible hazards that threaten success: pirates, sudden storms, rocky coastlines, and even mutiny. But the biggest danger of all is veering off course into an endless sea because you cannot plot your location accurately on the map.

Before John Harrison developed a special clock called the marine chronometer in the mid-1700s, sailors could not pinpoint their longitude—their location east or west of the prime meridian. Captains routinely lost hundreds of men and tons of cargo to starvation and storms while searching for a place to land. In Dava Sobel's wonderful book Longitude, *the author describes a dozen disasters,* including that of Admiral Sir Clowdisley Shovell. The admiral lost four of his five warships and 2,000 troops in 1707 after misjudging his longitude in the Scilly Isles, off the southwestern tip of England. Adrift in dense fog, the ships "pricked themselves on rocks and went down like stones." Yikes!

Fortunately, Harrison's ingenious clock enabled navigators to determine longitude by comparing the time of day on board ship with noon in Greenwich, England, which was (and still is) located on the prime meridian (0° longitude). Because latitude—the distance north or south of the Equator—was easy to calculate by observing the stars, sailors could now see where their latitude and longitude intersected on the map and determine their exact geographic location in an open ocean where there are no landmarks. (You'll learn more about latitude and longitude in Chapter 3.)

Early continental explorers also suffered when they lacked geographical information. Poor Hannibal crossed the Alps in the wrong time of year and nearly froze to death. Lewis and Clark almost perished in the mountains of Idaho and Montana because they didn't know how vast the Rocky Mountains were. And what were those Vikings thinking when they attempted to grow barley in Iceland a thousand years ago?

Knowing where places are located is an important first step to learning geography and enjoying the Bee. Fortunately for us, using maps and finding latitude and longitude are much easier today than during poor Sir Clowdisley Shovell's lifetime.

However, geography is much more than places on a map. In the words of Alexander Graham Bell, one of the founders of the

National Geographic Society, geography is "the world and all that is in it." Place-names such as Brazil, Stockholm, Mount Everest, and the Yangtze River are to geography what the alphabet is to reading. They open the gate for boundless and lifelong learning. Knowing where places are on a map is important, but the real heart of geography is understanding why people settled in a particular place, who their neighbors are, how they make a living, why they dress and speak the way they do, and what they do for fun. Developing this sense of place will raise a flat map to life.

Geographers investigate our global climate, landforms, economies, political systems, human cultures, and migration patterns. They are concerned not just with where something is located, but also with why it is there and how it relates to other things. A good geographer knows how to combine this information from many different sources and how to identify patterns that can help us understand our complex world. Geography explains why your grandmother moved to Tucson (warm and dry climate), how oil from Kuwait reaches Italy (by way of the Suez Canal), where tropical rain forests grow (near the Equator), who faces toward Mecca as they pray (Muslims), and which continent is the most populated (Asia). In a nutshell, geography is the "Why of Where" science that blends and enriches history, literature, mathematics, and science.

Although place-names of the world are now thoroughly mapped and available in atlases, maps, books, and even on-line, knowing where you are and the geographic characteristics of that place are just as important today as in earlier times.

Understanding people and environments influences the location of everything from Wal-marts to hospitals to software manufacturing plants. City planners need population projections and environmental data before they can approve plans to build housing developments, office buildings, and shopping centers. Engineers must study water resources and the lay of the land before starting any project (even a small hill or creek can greatly increase construction costs). Imagine trying to advertise a new product without knowing the composition (Hispanic, African American, Asian, European), age structure (teenagers or grandparents), and economic characteristics (farmers, factory workers, or professionals) of the people you want to buy it. Highway construction cannot proceed until facts about climate, soil, vegetation, and the number of people who will drive the proposed route are considered. Each day, kids everywhere awake in sheets of woven Egyptian cotton, pull on clothes stitched in Bangladesh, wolf down bananas grown in Central America, and grab schoolbooks printed in Singapore to board buses assembled in Michigan from parts made in Japan and Germany.

During the past decade, the growth of our global society—the rising dependence of nations upon each other for trade and security—has made geographical studies more important than ever. Acronyms and abbreviations, such as NAFTA, GATT, EU, and WTO, are heard on the evening news. Schools from Alaska to Zambia stress second-language and culture studies to better prepare their students not just for a global economy but for a more crowded planet where migration, tourism, and the Internet connect our global family more each day. America's War on Terrorism further underscores the great importance of more fully understanding the people of the world, how they live, what they believe, and the environment and resources we share.

Whether you are the secretary of state for the United States or the secretary of your class, knowing geography will help you understand the world.

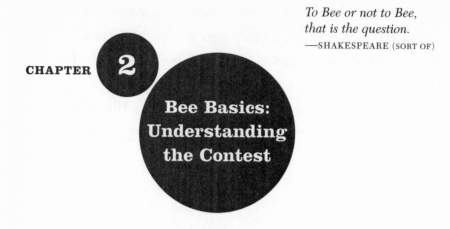

To Bee or not to Bee,
that is the question.
—SHAKESPEARE (SORT OF)

CHAPTER **2**

Bee Basics: Understanding the Contest

This chapter marches through the annual Bee calendar from Registration to the National Finals. It explains who is eligible to participate and the format at the school, state, and national levels. (It is important to note that although the Bee provides an instruction booklet to each registered school, the booklet contains recommended procedures only. Schools sometimes have to make adjustments to fit their needs.) Understanding how the Bee works and following the advice at the end of the chapter will help you relax, have fun, and perform better.

REGISTRATION

Registering is easy. Although only principals may register their schools, students (or their parents) can often stir teachers and principals into action! Check with school officials to see if your school is entered for the upcoming Bee. If you are a middle school student who rotates among classes, the social studies teacher is your best bet, followed by the principal. Schools must register *each* year by the October 15 deadline. More information on Bee registration appears on page 121, or check out www.nationalgeographic.com/geographicbee.

ELIGIBILITY

All U.S. schools with any of the grades four through eight may register for the Bee. Students enrolled in a conventional public or private school may not compete as part of a homeschool Bee. Homeschooling associations may register as a group to have a Bee. A student may compete in a magnet school Bee only if enrolled as a full-time student at the magnet school. (A student enrolled just part-time at a magnet school may not compete in the magnet school Bee.) Parents and teachers must pay close attention to these details to prevent a disqualification.

Students in grades four through eight who are not over the age of 15 at the time of the school-level competition in any given year may participate. The Bee is an open contest that does not separate students into age or grade-level categories. There must be a minimum of six student participants in a school to hold a school-level competition.

SCHOOL-LEVEL BEES

In mid November, the Society mails Bee packets to each registered school. The packet contains the suggested procedures, the question booklets, and prizes, including a Certificate of Participation for each student who takes part. School officials then select the days for their Bee, so long as the competition falls within the dates established by the Society—normally anytime between mid-November and mid-January.

The School Bees are usually broken into a Preliminary Competition, which normally takes place in individual classrooms, and the Final Competition, which is often held in the school assembly room (cafeteria, auditorium, gym, etc.).

Preliminary Competition

These rounds usually require an oral response. A teacher or other moderator reads the questions aloud. You will be asked one question per round and will have 15 seconds to answer each question. To keep the contest moving, you are allowed to ask to have a question repeated or a word spelled only two times during the Preliminary Competition. You should ask the moderator immediately if you want to interrupt the competition for either of these reasons.

Once the question has been repeated or the word spelled, you will have the remainder of your 15 seconds to answer the question. You must answer within the allotted time. No answer or an answer given after the 15 seconds is counted as a miss. One point is awarded for each correct response; a pass is counted as an incorrect response. There is no penalty for mispronunciations (or misspellings, in the event of a written response) so long as the moderator can determine you know the correct answer. The student with the most correct answers wins the chance to advance to the Final Round.

Tiebreakers

If there are ties in determining the finalists, school officials will use a series of Preliminary Competition Tiebreaker Questions. Everyone involved begins with a clean slate—no hits and no misses. Students get the same question and write their answers on the paper provided. Again, there is no penalty for misspellings so long as the moderator can determine that the correct answer has been given. Questioning continues until the tie or ties have been broken.

Final Competition

The Final Competition consists of a Final Round and a Championship Round. If you are lucky enough to advance to this level, you may find yourself on a stage in the school auditorium. As with any contest or game, the pressure builds as you progress up the ladder. Expect some bright lights and audience noise, ranging from restrained gasps to thunderous applause.

In addition to the round-robin oral questions you encountered in the Preliminary Competition, the Final Round includes questions that require written responses (students are simultaneously asked the same question and respond by writing their answers on the paper provided). Other questions may involve graphs, maps, or photographs. If so, you will be given a copy of the visual to study up close before answering the question. But the biggest difference between the Preliminary Competition and the Final Round is that students are eliminated after giving their second incorrect answer. Once the third-place winner has been determined, the remaining two students advance to the Championship Round.

Championship Round

The Championship Round involves three questions. The two contestants start with a clean slate. Both are asked the same questions simultaneously and given 15 seconds to write their answers. The moderator then asks the students for their answers. The student with the most correct answers wins the School Bee. Tiebreaker questions may be necessary to determine the winner. The champion receives a prize and certificate from the National Geographic Society, and every student who entered the School Bee receives a Certificate of Participation.

QUALIFYING TEST

To advance to the State Bee, the school winner must take the written Qualifying Test. This test should be given in a quiet location in the school building. It must be monitored by a teacher who is not a parent or guardian of the School Bee winner. There are about 70 multiple-choice questions that sweep across the entire range of geographic inquiry, including a set that pertains to a map, table, or graph. There is a time limit of one hour. When time is up, the teacher administering the test must sign the certification statement on the answer sheet and mail it to the National Geographic Society. The test must be postmarked by January 15 and received by the Society no later than January 31 of the year of the test. Faxes are not accepted.

The National Geographic Society scores one Qualifying Test from each participating school. The top 100 students (more if there are ties) from each of the 50 states, the District of

Columbia, the Department of Defense Dependents Schools, the Virgin Islands, Puerto Rico, and the Pacific territories compete in the State Bees. The National Geographic Society appoints State Bee Coordinators to administer this portion of the contest. In early March, Society officials notify the teachers of the students who qualify for the State Competition.

STATE-LEVEL BEES

The State Bees are usually held in early April. An adult must accompany each student to the State Bee. In most cases this is a teacher, parent, or legal guardian. Other adults may substitute with school approval. Expect the Bee to begin with an opening assembly jam-packed with all 100 State Finalists, officials, teachers, and a zillion family members. The room is abuzz with excitement and nervous anticipation.

The contestants break into five groups of 20 students. The seating and room assignments are determined by random drawing before the Bee. Just as in the school-level competition, there are preliminary, final, and championship rounds (and tiebreakers if necessary). The Final and Championship Rounds are held in front of a large audience and are very exciting. Plan to attend even if you don't qualify to participate. Once the pressure is off, you will impress yourself with how many questions you can answer correctly! The same procedure that is recommended to schools for determining the school-level winners is used to determine the state champions. The winner of each State Bee wins a trip to Washington, D.C., to compete in the National-Level Bee.

THE NATIONAL-LEVEL BEE

State Bee winners meet at the headquarters of the National Geographic Society, in Washington, D.C., in late May to compete for the title of National Champion. The national-level format is similar to that of the previous levels of the Bee except that the questions are harder and there are more rounds involving visuals, such as photographs, maps, and graphs. Also, in the Final and Championship Rounds you have only 12 seconds to answer each question. The top ten winners of the Preliminary Competition compete in the Final Round. Alex Trebek, host of TV's *JEOPARDY!*, has moderated the Final and Championship Rounds since 1989. These rounds are now carried on the National Geographic Channel and most PBS stations. Check your local listings, and follow along with the national finalists to see how many questions you can answer. The top three finishers take home college scholarships. The total prize and scholarship monies awarded at the school, state, and national levels make the Bee one of the richest academic competitions for schoolkids on Earth.

THE GREAT CANADIAN GEOGRAPHY CHALLENGE

The Canadian equivalent of the National Geographic Bee also features a series of competitions at the school, provincial or territorial, and national levels that are designed to test students' knowledge and skills in geography.

Currently there are two grade levels to the Challenge: Level 1 for grades four to six and Level 2 for grades seven and above. All Level 2 competitors must be under the age of 16 as of June 30 (the end of the school year in which the Challenge takes place). Only schools, not individuals, may register for the Challenge, and any number of students or classes within a school may compete. All registered schools receive an instruction booklet, a question and answer booklet, and prizes. The kits are available in English and French.

The competition for Level 1 students ends at the school level; Level 2 students with the top 50 scores on the written qualifying test in each province or territory are invited to a Provincial or Territorial Challenge, held in April. The highest-scoring students from this competition compete for the National Final in May. The top three scorers are declared the Canadian National Champions and receive college scholarships.

BEE GREAT: ADVICE TO CONTESTANTS

The following list is the result of more than a decade of "Bee-ing" with students, teachers, and parents. Although my experience has been mostly at the state level, these tips will help at any level in almost any type of competition. They are included here to help make the Bee a truly memorable and fun event.

Relax! Cramming hurts your brain

The evening before and the morning of the Bee are prime times to relax, play with your dog, and bike ride with a sibling or friend. Don't stay up the night before conversing with owls while attempting to cram in a few last-minute facts. This contest is fun, so rest up and dream of faraway lands.

Set aside part of each day to prepare for the Bee. Remember that geography is an integrative subject that takes time to learn and appreciate. Avoid flipping flash cards on the way to the Bee. (Several times I have seen parents quizzing students just moments before the Bee!) This adds tension that can detract from the quality of your performance and your enjoyment of the competition.

Healthy body, healthy mind

Whether you live in Paris, Pyongyang, or Philadelphia, the best advice is to stay fit, eat a balanced diet, and avoid spending so much time on-line and with books that your physical fitness declines. A healthy body houses a sharper and more capable mind.

Many students at every level of the Bee find that eating before the contest is a difficult idea to stomach. Yet your brain is a big muscle, and to keep it working at full throttle requires high-octane fuel. That is to say, CHOW DOWN BEFORE THE BEE! Don't arrive hungry. An empty stomach will make any jitters you have feel much worse. This problem does not affect every student, but if you know that big events—however much fun they may be—make it difficult to eat, then here is some food for thought.

First, eat a well-balanced dinner the night before the Bee. This way, unless your stomach is the size of a thimble, you'll have calories in your tank at least through noon the following day. Second, eat at least a small breakfast that includes some juice and something solid, such as fruit, carbohydrates (toast, muffins, cereal), or eggs. Try to avoid greasy and high-fat foods, as they are harder to digest and can make your tummy do back flips.

Dress for success

Although this is a special event, you don't need to rent a tux or a frilly evening gown. Even ties and dresses are rare. Most kids—both girls and boys—pull on something comfortable. Pants or a skirt with a clean shirt or blouse are a good choice. Of course, you'll want to look neat. Remember that advancing to the finals at any level could land you onstage.

Take a deep breath

It's easy to panic when you hear a question that freaks you out! "Oh no, I can't remember the largest city on Mars!" Forgetting to breathe or taking several gasps is a natural reaction. If this occurs during the Bee, relax, take a deep breath, collect your thoughts, and then look for clues in the question that will help you figure out the correct answer. Remember, you have 15 seconds (except in the National Finals) to answer each question. Believe it or not, that's a long time! Failing to take in oxygen will make it more difficult to think and will increase that feeling of alarm!

Listen to every question in each round

When competing in the oral rounds, listen to every question and every answer. You may pick up clues that will help you come up with the right answer when it's your turn.

Stand by your first answer

Unless you are certain of an error, stick with the first answer that comes to mind. Believe it or not, studies show that students who change their answers or get stuck trying to choose between two answers usually select a less accurate choice the second time.

Ignore your friends

While you're competing, don't look at people you know, especially just before and during your turn. Ask your friends, teacher, parents, and other family members to make themselves invisible by sitting as far away as possible. Also, tell them to photograph you *after* the Bee, not while you are trying to remember which country borders Zimbabwe on the east. (Mozambique, of course!)

Speak loudly and write with a big stick

Make your answers known in very decisive ways. Speak in a loud, clear voice. When a written answer is required, write clearly in LARGE, BOLD LETTERS. The teacher/moderator must be able to understand your answer and read your handwriting.

Remember: It is impossible to fail in the Bee. Just by taking part you are already a success!

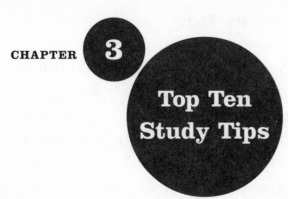

CHAPTER **3**

Top Ten Study Tips

*All the rivers
run into the sea;
yet the sea is not full;
Unto the place
from whence
the rivers come,
thither they return
again.*
—ECCLESIASTES

The ten trusty tips outlined in this chapter will help you "Bee" ready. This powerful advice has been assembled over many years from students just like you. A small army of teachers added their two cents' worth, too.

Don't expect to learn everything about geography in just one school year. Remember that you are eligible to enter the Bee from the fourth through the eighth grade. No one expects a fourth grader to know as much as an eighth grader, but it's not impossible. Susannah Batko-Yovino was only a sixth grader when she became the National Champion in 1990! By participating each year, you will increase your knowledge of geography and self-confidence. These ten study tips will teach you the basics and how to build on them to recognize geographic patterns. You'll be thinking like a geographer in no time!

TIP

Choose Your Tools

Getting started in geography is easy if you have the right tools. Spending a part of each day with these tools will expand your world in a hurry. A few pointers on using these are presented here. You'll find advice about specific products and where to find them in Chapter 6.

A large **WORLD MAP** should be in every home. Concentrate first on learning the continents, oceans, and largest islands. Then focus on countries, capital cities, and major physical features (such as mountain ranges, lakes, and rivers), gradually adding other places and features to your vocabulary. Hang your world map next to your bed or on the closet door. Put smaller maps of each continent around your house. Position one in the bathroom so you can learn the countries of Africa while brushing your teeth. Laminated map placemats let you explore Italy while slurping spaghetti. You can also tape maps behind the front seat of your family car and visit South America on the way to school.

A good **ATLAS** is the next essential tool. These come in all sizes, with many excellent and reasonably priced volumes to match your skill level. Be sure to use one that is less than five years old so that it includes important name updates.

Look for three other features when choosing an atlas. First, it should have both physical maps (emphasizing natural features) and political maps (emphasizing country boundaries and cities). Second, make sure it includes an index (or gazetteer) that alphabetically lists place-names that appear on the maps. This will help you find unfamiliar locations. Finally, look for text that includes information about each continent, country, and world region (such as Southeast Asia or Middle America), plus a section on geographic comparisons (longest rivers, largest cities, etc.).

BLANK OUTLINE MAPS are the third item for your kit. These black-and-white line maps outline the continents and countries. Important physical features such as major rivers and mountain ranges may also appear. Use these to practice labeling countries, cities, rivers, lakes, mountains, islands, and other geographic information as you learn it. Always start with the most obvious features, then add more detailed information as you progress. Blank outline maps are a great way to quiz your growing knowledge of the world. Several on-line sources are listed in Chapter 6.

A **GEOGRAPHY REFERENCE BOOK** rounds out your tool kit. Although maps and atlases help you learn where Mongolia, Mauna Loa, and other places are located, a good geography reference book explains *why* they are located there, *who* lives there, *what* they do, and *how* the landscape came to be. These books usually arrange information in alphabetical order either by single topic (Agriculture, Alluvial Fan, Avalanche), or by category (Earth Science, Population, Wildlife). The most helpful ones enrich the text with numerous maps, photographs, charts and graphs, and a glossary of terms. A good reference book takes you to the next level of geographic learning by raising flat maps to life. This marks the point where memorization evolves into real geographic exploration and discovery!

TIP #2 Learn the Language of Maps

A good map is worth a thousand pictures. Expert map readers can absorb oceans of geographic information in a short time. But to understand all that a map can tell you, you must first learn the language of maps.

LATITUDE and **LONGITUDE** are the imaginary lines that divide Earth's surface into a grid. Under this system, both latitude and longitude are measured in terms of the 360 degrees of a circle. The latitude and longitude of a place are its **COORDINATES**. Coordinates mark the **ABSOLUTE LOCATION** of a place. Understanding coordinates, you can use a map to locate any point on Earth.

Latitude is the distance north or south of the **EQUATOR**, the line of 0° latitude that divides the Earth into two equal halves called hemispheres. The top half is the **NORTHERN HEMISPHERE**, and the bottom half is the **SOUTHERN HEMISPHERE**. Lines of latitude are also called **PARALLELS** because they circle the Earth without ever touching each other. From the Equator we measure latitude north and south to the Poles. The **NORTH POLE** is located at 90°N latitude, and the **SOUTH POLE** is located at 90°S latitude.

There are other important parallels that you should learn. The parallel of latitude $23^{1}/_{2}°$ north of the Equator is called the **TROPIC OF CANCER**, and the parallel $23^{1}/_{2}°$ south of the Equator is the **TROPIC OF CAPRICORN**. Any location between these two parallels is called the **TROPICS**. The **SUBTROPICS** are the zones located between 23$^{1/2}$° and about 40° north and south of the Equator.

The parallel of latitude 66$^{1/2}$° north of the Equator is called the **ARCTIC CIRCLE**, and the line 66$^{1/2}$° south of the Equator is the **ANTARCTIC CIRCLE**. The region between 66$^{1/2}$°N and 90°N is called the Arctic; the region between 66$^{1/2}$°S and 90°S is called the Antarctic. Both regions can simply be called polar.

Longitude is the distance east or west of the **PRIME MERIDIAN**, the point of 0° longitude. This is also the starting place for measuring distance both east and west around the globe. Lines of longitude are called **MERIDIANS**. They also circle Earth, but connect with each other at the Poles.

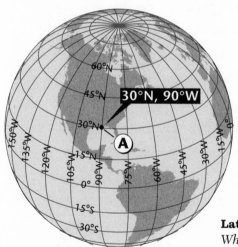

Latitude and Longitude
When used together, latitude and longitude form a grid that provides a system for determining the exact, or absolute, location of every place on Earth. For example, the absolute location of point A is 30°N, 90°W.

We also use the coordinate system to determine direction. When you face the North Pole (90°N), the sun rises to your right (east) and sets to your left (west). The south is behind you. These four points—north, south, east, and west—are **CARDINAL DIRECTIONS**. Any point *between* two cardinal directions is an **INTERMEDIATE DIRECTION**. For example, looking north and partly to the east is said to be looking northeast. But if you turn around and glance south and partly to the west, you are looking southwest.

A **GLOBE** is the only accurate representation of our spherical Earth. Think of a globe as a scale model of Earth with a paper or plastic map mounted on its spherical surface. Globes are great to study because unlike most flat maps, they show continents and oceans in their true proportions. Size, shape, distance, and direction are all accurately represented. Projecting this round shape onto a flat sheet of paper to make a map distorts these elements.

To solve the problem of distortion, mapmakers use a variety of **MAP PROJECTIONS** to portray our curved Earth on a flat sheet of paper. Each projection distorts the Earth according to a mathematical calculation. Three commonly used projections are the Mercator, the Winkel Tripel, and the Goode's Interrupted Homolosine. The **MERCATOR** projection is helpful to navigators because it allows them to maintain a constant compass direction as they travel between two points, but it greatly exaggerates areas at higher latitudes. The **WINKEL TRIPEL** is a general purpose projection popularly used for political, physical, and thematic maps because it minimizes distortion of both size and shape. The

GOODE'S INTERRUPTED HOMOLOSINE minimizes distortion of scale and shape by interrupting the globe. This type of equal-area projection is useful for mapping comparisons of various kinds of data, such as rain forests and population density.

MERCATOR

WINKEL TRIPEL

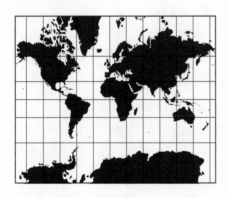

GOODE'S INTERRUPTED HOMOLOSINE

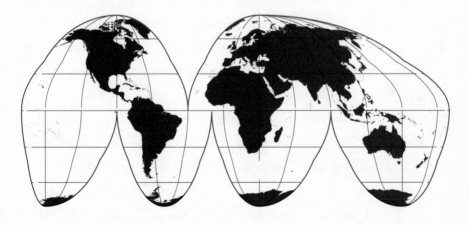

There are two main types of maps. **PHYSICAL MAPS** emphasize natural features such as mountains, rivers, lakes, deserts, and plains. Mapmakers often use shades of color to indicate different elevations. **POLITICAL MAPS** use lines to show boundaries between countries, points to show cities, and various other symbols to show roads, airports, canals, and other human-related features. Examples of these two kinds of maps are on the facing page.

We use longitude and latitude to determine the absolute location of physical and political features and **RELATIVE LOCATION** to explain the underlying reasons for that precise location and to show the interconnection of geographic phenomena.

For example, the geographic grid pinpoints Chicago's absolute location at 41°N latitude, 87°W longitude. However, the Windy City's location on the shore of Lake Michigan is *relative* to the historic water commerce routes favored by early Native Americans and settlers. Without Lake Michigan, Chicago might not exist.

Similarly, Khartoum, the capital city of Sudan, is located at 15°N latitude, 32°E longitude, *relative* to the confluence of the Blue and the White Nile. Without this confluence of rivers, this city out in the center of the Sahara would not have become such an important economic center.

Physical features are located relative to the geologic processes that created them. For example, Mount Rainier, in Washington State, is located at 47°N latitude, 122°W longitude, relative to the collision of two tectonic plates (moving slabs of Earth's crust) that created the Cascade Range. As a result, Mount Rainier shares the same geologic origin as the other volcanoes located north and

PHYSICAL MAP

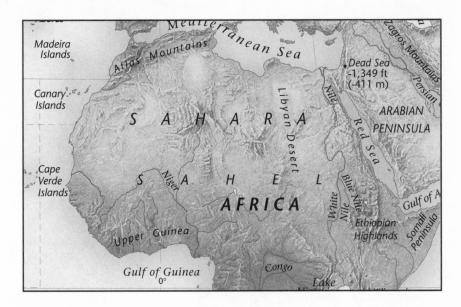

POLITICAL MAP

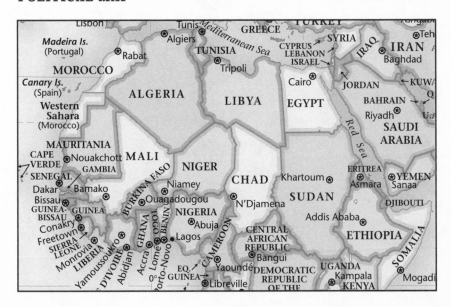

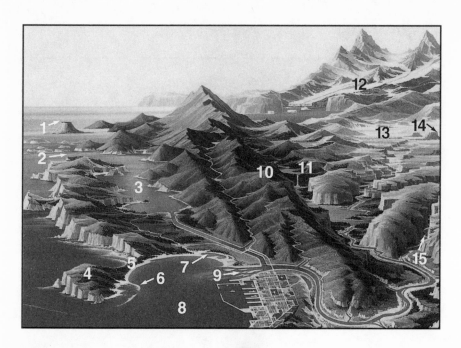

IMAGINARY LANDSCAPE

1	Volcano	**8**	Bay
2	Strait	**9**	Delta
3	Sound	**10**	Divide
4	Peninsula	**11**	Reservoir
5	Isthmus	**12**	Glacier
6	Spit	**13**	Desert
7	Lagoon	**14**	Mesa
		15	Canyon

south of it. Without the tectonic plate boundary, this part of the Pacific Northwest would have a much different physical environment and human settlement pattern than we see today.

Use the world maps, atlases, and geographic reference books in your tool kit to learn more about these concepts and the language of maps. They are the building blocks for more learning and the source of many Bee questions.

The diagram of an imaginary landscape on the facing page was used in a round of questions in a State-Level Bee to quiz students on their ability to identify physical features. Students were asked to give the number that best represented a specific physical feature. Of course, they didn't have the benefit of being able to see the answers! They are provided for you so that you can use this as a study tool for learning some very basic physical terms. You will find definitions for each of these terms in your geographical reference book. Learn them and try to find examples of each on physical maps. You can be sure that geographic terms are a frequent topic for Bee questions.

Once you know how to read maps, the next step is to learn the most important place-names that go on them. This memorization develops your global sense of place. Learning place-names is like learning your ABCs. Without knowing the alphabet, you can't spell words. Without knowing place-names, you can't identify places and features on a map or understand the interrelationships between physical and human activities. They are a necessary and important building block to greater geographic knowledge.

The number of place-names can be overwhelming. Organizing them into physical and political groups can be helpful. Start with the first categories in each group and work your way down. Don't just memorize a list of names and figures. Find each feature or place on the map and take time to learn about it and what it's near.

PHYSICAL FEATURES

THE CONTINENTS

	AREA (sq mi)	(sq km)	Percent of Earth's Land
Asia	17,212,000	44,579,000	30.0
Africa	11,608,000	30,065,000	20.2
North America	9,366,500	24,256,000	16.5
South America	6,880,500	17,819,000	12.0
Antarctica	5,100,400	13,209,000	8.9
Europe	3,837,000	9,938,000	6.7
Australia	2,968,000	7,687,000	5.2

THE OCEANS

	AREA (sq mi)	(sq km)	% of Earth's Water Area
Pacific	64,186,671	166,241,000	46.0
Atlantic	33,420,000	86,557,000	23.9
Indian	28,350,000	73,427,000	20.3
Arctic	3,662,800	9,485,000	2.6

Note: Although some geographers consider Europe and Asia as one continent called Eurasia, National Geographic counts them as two landmasses to make a total of seven continents. Likewise, some maps show a Southern Ocean around Antarctica. In reality this body of water is just the continuation of the Atlantic, Pacific, and Indian Oceans. The tables at the bottom of the previous page list the names of the continents and oceans in order by size.

HIGHEST POINT ON EACH CONTINENT

	feet	meters
Everest, Asia	29,035	8,850
Aconcagua, South America	22,834	6,960
McKinley (Denali), N. America	20,320	6,194
Kilimanjaro, Africa	19,340	5,895
El'brus, Europe	18,510	5,642
Vinson Massif, Antarctica	16,067	4,897
Kosciuszko, Australia	7,310	2,228

LOWEST POINT ON EACH CONTINENT

	feet	meters
Dead Sea, Asia	-1,365	-416
Lake Assal, Africa	-512	-156
Death Valley, N. America	-282	-86
Valdés Peninsula, S. America	-131	-40
Caspian Sea, Europe	-92	-28
Lake Eyre, Australia	-52	-16
Antarctica (ice covered)	-8,366	-2,550

TEN LARGEST SEAS

	AREA	
	(sq mi)	(sq km)
South China	1,148,500	2,974,600
Caribbean	971,400	2,515,900
Mediterranean	969,100	2,510,000
Bering	873,000	2,261,100
Gulf of Mexico	582,100	1,507,600
Sea of Okhotsk	537,500	1,392,100
Sea of Japan	391,100	1,012,900
Hudson Bay	281,900	730,100
East China	256,600	664,600
Andaman	218,100	564,900

TEN LARGEST LAKES

	AREA	
	(sq mi)	(sq km)
Caspian Sea, Europe-Asia	143,200	371,000
Superior, N. America	31,700	82,100
Victoria, Africa	26,800	69,500
Huron, N. America	23,000	59,600
Michigan, N. America	22,300	57,800
Tanganyika, Africa	12,600	32,600
Baikal, Asia	12,200	31,500
Great Bear, N. America	12,100	31,300
Aral Sea, Asia	11,900	30,700
Malawi, Africa	11,200	28,900

TEN LARGEST ISLANDS

	AREA				AREA	
	(sq mi)	(sq km)			(sq mi)	(sq km)
Greenland	840,000	2,175,600	Sumatra		165,000	427,300
New Guinea	306,000	792,500	Honshu		87,800	227,400
Borneo	280,100	725,100	Great Britain		84,200	218,100
Madagascar	226,600	587,000	Victoria		83,900	217,300
Baffin	196,000	507,500	Ellesmere		75,800	196,200

LONGEST RIVERS*

	miles	kilometers
Nile, Africa	4,241	6,825
Amazon, S. America	4,000	6,437
Yangtze (Chang), Asia	3,964	6,380
Mississippi-Missouri, N. America	3,710	5,971
Murray-Darling, Australia	2,310	3,718
Volga, Europe	2,290	3,685

Antarctica has no flowing rivers

* These lists name the longest river and the major
  mountain range on each continent.

MAJOR MOUNTAIN RANGES*

Alps, Europe

Andes, South America

Atlas Mountains, Africa

Great Dividing Range, Australia

Himalaya, Asia

Rocky Mountains, North America

Transantarctic Mountains, Antarctica

Ural Mountains form much of the boundary
between Europe and Asia

EARTH'S EXTREMES

Hottest Place: Dalol, Denakil Depression, Ethiopia;
annual average temperature—93°F (34°C)
Coldest Place: Plateau Station, Antarctica;
annual average temperature— -70°F (-56.7°C)
Wettest Place: Mawsynram, Assam, India;
annual average rainfall—467 in (1,187.3 cm)
Driest Place: Atacama Desert, Chile; rainfall
barely measurable
Highest Waterfall: Angel Falls, Venezuela;
3,212 ft (979 m)

Largest Desert: Sahara, Africa; 3,475,000 sq mi
(9,000,000 sq km)
Largest Canyon: Grand Canyon, Colorado River,
Arizona; 277 mi (446 km) long along the river;
1,801 ft (549 m) to 18 mi (29 km) wide; about 1 mi
(1.6 km) deep
Longest Reef: Great Barrier Reef, Australia;
1,250 mi (2,012 km)
Greatest Tides: Bay of Fundy, Nova Scotia,
Canada—52 ft (16 m)

THE POLITICAL WORLD

Most atlases list countries with statistical information, such as area and population, so that you can make your own chart of the largest and smallest by area and by population. Although area figures seldom change (unless there is boundary change), population figures do. Use Web sites listed in Chapter 6 to keep up-to-date.

The countries of North America: North America is made up of 23 independent countries. It includes Canada, the United States, Mexico, the countries of Central America, the islands of the West Indies, and Greenland.

The countries of South America: South America is made up of 12 independent countries and one French territory, French Guiana.

The countries of Europe: Russia is usually counted as one of Europe's 43 independent countries. Although most of its land is in Asia, most of its people and its capital city (Moscow) are west of the Ural Mountains in Europe.

The countries of Africa: Africa has 53 independent countries. Most people live along the Nile and south of the Sahara.

The countries of Asia: China is the largest country located entirely in Asia and also the most populous of Asia's 46 countries.

Australia, New Zealand, and Oceania: Australia is a continent and a country. Geographers often include it and New Zealand with the islands of the south and central Pacific and call this region Oceania. Australia is the largest and most populous of the 14 independent countries in this region.

Antarctica: This is the only continent that has no independent countries and no permanent population.

Master Mental Maps

Studying geographic shapes and place-names will eventually fix mental maps in your brain. You'll be able to picture not only where a place is, but what's near it, who lives there, and lots more. The ability to produce mental images of the world characterizes all Bee champions. This requires atlas and reference book use and a good understanding of map scale.

MAP SCALE makes it possible to figure out what distance on Earth's surface is represented by a given length on a map. Large-scale maps show a limited geographic area such as a neighborhood or city in great detail. The scale on such a map may be expressed as the ratio 1:1,500, meaning that every inch on the map equals 1,500 inches on the ground. (You might try crawling 1,500 inches to see how far it really is.) This allows the cartographer to include street names, parks, and creeks. A large-scale map of the United States wouldn't fit in your backpack. In fact, you'd need a dump truck!

Small-scale maps have much less detail but cover a greater geographical area, such as a state, mountain range, or continent. The scale here may read 1:5,000,000 (one inch equals five million inches on the ground—a very long crawl). This level of detail is the only way to cover a large area such as a continent or the world so that you can study it as a whole.

The next step is adding more physical and cultural depth to these mental maps. The following categories will get you started.

PHYSICAL FEATURES

Vegetation Zones, or Biomes: There are four main categories of vegetation zones: forest, grassland, desert, and tundra. Start with these, then expand your knowledge by learning about the different types of vegetation within these categories. Vegetation is closely linked to climate.

Climate Zones: Climate is the long-term average weather conditions of a place. Most climate maps show at least five different zones: tropical, dry, temperate, continental, and polar. As you build your knowledge, you will become familiar with subcategories, such as tropical wet and dry, arid and semiarid, marine west coast, and Mediterranean.

CULTURAL FEATURES

Population Density: Population density is the number of people living in each square mile or kilometer of a place. The population density of a country is calculated by dividing its population by its area. Asia is the most densely populated continent; Australia is the least densely populated continent (excluding Antarctica). Check out your maps and see if you can figure out why!

Religion: All of the world's major religions—Christianity, Hinduism, Judaism, Buddhism, Islam—as well as Shinto, Taoism, and Confucianism originated in Asia. They spread around the world as people migrated to new areas.

Languages: There are thousands of languages, but there are only 12 major language families. Languages in the Indo-European family, which includes English, Russian, and German, are spoken over the widest geographic area. Mandarin Chinese is spoken by the most people. Can you figure out why?

ECONOMIC FEATURES

World Economy: Familiarize yourself with terms such as primary, secondary, tertiary, and quaternary, as well as developed and developing, industrialized and nonindustrialized.

Commerce: Learn the major crops, minerals, and products that countries on each continent produce and export. Then take note of major trade alliances, such as NAFTA (North American Free Trade Agreement), the EU (European Union), WTO (World Trade Organization), and OPEC (Organization of Petroleum Exporting Countries).

Transportation: Study maps, charts, and graphs to learn about major trade routes by land, sea, and air.

Filling in your mental maps will take some time, so be patient. Find a study method that works for you and then hop to it!

TIP #5 Build Your Knowledge

Conquering place-names prepares you to tackle the biggest and most rewarding challenge of preparing for the Bee: learning about the world's primary physical and cultural patterns. Understanding how the world functions as an interconnected and dynamic system is what geography is all about. Studying these patterns prepares you to combine and layer more complex geographic information onto your basic mental maps. This takes time, but the rewards are great. The following suggestions are designed to help you reach this level.

COMBINE INFORMATION

Good geographers combine information from different sources to arrive at logical conclusions. They understand the basic patterns of climate, geology, vegetation, human settlement, migration, and commerce. Combining these patterns with a knowledge of regions and place-names will empower you to answer very specific questions that otherwise might have been a choice between two guesses. At the very least it will enable you to make an educated guess when you don't know the answer. The question analyses that follow explain how this works.

1. Which city recently suffered a severe earthquake, Tokyo or Omaha?

You may not recall any recent earthquakes, but you know that Tokyo is in Japan, an island country off the east coast of Asia, along the tectonic Ring of Fire. Omaha is a city in Nebraska, a state located in the middle of the North American plate. Since more earthquakes occur around the rim of the Pacific Ocean than anywhere else, you correctly answer **Tokyo**.

2. Which is Germany's most important export crop, wheat or palm oil?

Using your mental maps, you know that Germany is a midlatitude country in western Europe. You also know that palm trees grow in warm tropical climates and that wheat grows in more temperate regions, like the American Midwest. Given Germany's location, you reason that it is more likely to have a temperate rather than a tropical climate, and you correctly answer **wheat**.

LEARN PATTERNS ON THE LAND

Interpreting a landscape is very different from memorizing names on a map. Geographers use **THEMATIC MAPS** to show patterns on the land. They start with a physical or a political base map and add layers of information to show whatever geographic theme they wish to emphasize—everything from world population and energy consumption *(see map opposite, top)* to shark attacks and local weather predictions.

    CARTOGRAMS are special kinds of thematic maps. On them, the size of a country is based on a statistic other than land area. In the cartogram shown, population determines the size of each country. This is why Nigeria, Africa's most populous country, is shown much larger than Sudan, Africa's largest country in area.

THEMATIC MAP

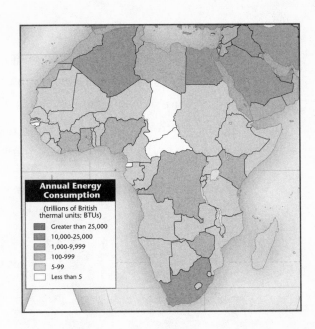

Annual Energy Consumption

(trillions of British thermal units: BTUs)

- Greater than 25,000
- 10,000-25,000
- 1,000-9,999
- 100-999
- 5-99
- Less than 5

CARTOGRAM

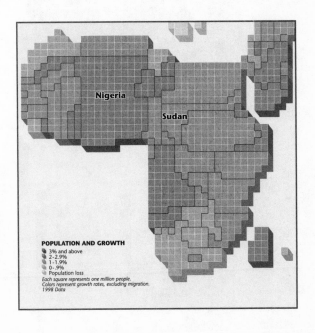

Nigeria

Sudan

POPULATION AND GROWTH
- 3% and above
- 2-2.9%
- 1-1.9%
- 0-.9%
- Population loss

Each square represents one million people.
Colors represent growth rates, excluding migration.
1998 Data

INTERPRETING GRAPHS

Graphs are another important tool that geographers use to convey information, and you can expect to encounter various kinds in the Bee. A special kind of bar graph called a population pyramid *(below, top)* shows the distribution of a country's population by sex and age. A more traditional style of bar graph shows water usage.

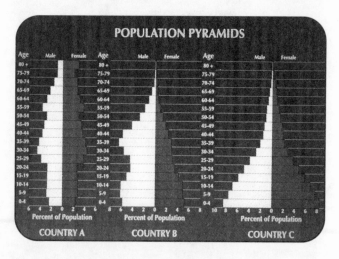

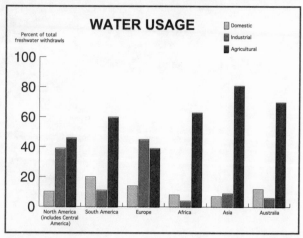

Make School Work for You

Geography is all around you! The first place to look is in school. History uniformly incorporates geography in discussing wars (the Russian winter froze the German Army in World War II), slavery (wind belts made the triangular trade possible), and ecological disasters (poor farming techniques and drought triggered the Dust Bowl during the 1930s). You will also find geography concepts in literature (Mark Twain, Robert Service, Laura Ingalls Wilder), science classes (especially Earth science and biology), mathematics (latitude and longitude, population studies, sun angles, etc.), and fine arts (dance, music, and paintings are all reflections of culture). You can even find geography in your school cafeteria (tacos, spaghetti, and rice). With good mental maps and the ability to combine information from different sources, you can spend your entire school day in excellent preparation for the Bee!

TIP #7 Use Your Geographic Eyes

When you can think like a geographer and understand the major patterns that influence our physical environment, culture, and economy, it's time for some field observation. The following suggestions will get your nose out of the books and into the real world.

BECOME AN OBSERVANT MALL RAT

Stores are filled with goods from every corner of the world. The origin of these products and their movement around the globe tells us much about where raw materials such as wood, minerals, and cotton come from, who makes them into finished products such as furniture, baseball bats, and shirts, and who buys them. They also furnish clues about labor use, population growth rates, and the huge difference in wealth between rich and poor countries.

Combining information from product labels and packaging with your mental maps represents advanced geographic thinking. You can practice this in stores, at school, and at home by reading the labels and packaging on products to find out where the raw materials used to make them came from and who made them.

For example, many computers are manufactured in China from European and Japanese components. They carry a U.S.A. label and are packaged in boxes made in Mexico. Most toys are manufactured in China. Much of our clothing is stitched in Mexico, Central America, or Asia. Many books are printed in

Singapore. After much practice, you will find it easier to predict which country names will appear on boxes and labels. This is great evidence that your mental maps are becoming more detailed!

Check out stores that sell furniture (look for exotic woods), electronics (identify manufactured goods with components from multiple regions), and indigenous art (that comes from every-where). A century ago, Americans prized goods made overseas for their exotic qualities. Today, it would be extraordinarily difficult to outfit a home with products made only in North America. Global connections are the heart of the world's economy.

STOMACH MORE GEOGRAPHY

Grocery stores offer products from everywhere. Look for New Zealand kiwis, Colombian coffee, Central Asian spices, Swiss chocolate, and Mexican avocados among the zillion other prod-ucts from around the world that arrive in your local food store.

Be aware that geographic place-names incorporated into prod-uct labels can sometimes lead you astray. For instance, check out fine china from Ireland, India ink bottled in South America, chili peppers grown in Mexico, English muffins baked from Nebraska wheat, and Canadian bacon from hogs raised in Iowa!

ATTEND COMMUNITY AND LOCAL EVENTS

Local communities are a great geographic resource. Keep an eye out for free concerts and lectures. Visit your museums and library display cases. If you have a college or university nearby, watch for public lectures and exhibits.

#8 Stay Current with Current Events

Current events questions query knowledge about natural disasters (the eruption of Mount Pinatubo, Mississippi flooding, earthquakes in Peru), political upheaval (civil wars in Africa, tensions between India and Pakistan, war in Afghanistan), international agreements (Kyoto Protocol, NAFTA, GATT), and discoveries (archaeological ruins, new plant species, Arctic oil, etc.). Almost any topic that is in the news, especially if it involves more than one of the categories mentioned above is fair game for the Bee. Stories that have been the subject of Bee questions include the spread of AIDS, the *Exxon Valdez* oil spill, the election of Nelson Mandela in South Africa, and China's Three Gorges Dam.

For our purposes, we can divide current events into ongoing topics—such as global warming and oil exploration—and breaking news stories, such as the World Trade Center attacks, the new European currency, and a hurricane or other natural disaster.

Your local and regional media (newspapers, TV, radio) are great ways to keep tabs on our rapidly changing world. On-line news sites are also good sources, and they report events from many different perspectives. You can scan on-line newspapers in a matter of minutes. They also offer great maps, photos, archived back issues, and links to related sites.

TIP #9 Read, Read, Read

Bee champions share a passion for reading. They read books, magazines, newspapers, cereal boxes, Web sites—anything they can lay their eyes on. They read at school, at grandma's, and on buses, trains, and airplanes. They read on weekends and throughout the summer. Reading helps build your mental maps of people and places around the world. At the same time, reading becomes more geographic once you have good mental maps that enliven and enrich almost any story or news item. You can add to your mental maps as you read by keeping a map handy. Use it to find new places and features and to understand relationships between the land and the people.

Chapter 6 evaluates several games that use a quiz format like the Bee's to test your knowledge of geography. The Bee Web site offers five new geography questions every day to give you an idea of what the questions in the contest are like.

Playing these games offers several advantages. First, they simulate the Bee by asking questions from diverse topics that require an answer in a fixed amount of time. Second, they can help you identify your weak areas so that you can concentrate on improving those skills. A final advantage is that many of these games require multiple players, which doubles the opportunity to learn, promotes discussion, and lets you benefit from the knowledge of others.

There are other kinds of fun and productive study aids. Some, such as flash cards, are helpful for testing basic facts. Others are great for gathering interesting geo-tidbits. These should be treated as supplements to your learning.

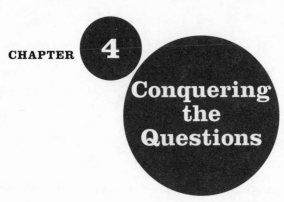

4

Conquering the Questions

Genius is one percent inspiration and ninety-nine percent perspiration.
—THOMAS ALVA EDISON

This chapter presents questions that have been used at the school, state, and national levels of the Bee. Most are from the preliminary competitions, as questions there are organized by geographic categories. Samples of map, graph, and photo questions are also included.

The objective here is not to provide questions and answers for you to memorize. Rather, it is to make you familiar with the kinds of questions asked in the Bee and show you how to look for clues within the questions that can help you come up with the right answers. Learning how to recognize the clues will reinforce the need to master the ten study tips outlined in Chapter 3. It is important to remember that the purpose of the Bee is to test your knowledge of geography. This means you don't have to worry about "trick" questions. Just take your time and think things through. Even if you answer incorrectly, you will learn something new for next time.

Before plunging into the questions, here are a few pointers to remember about the real contest. First, remember the Bee is an oral competition (except for the written Qualifying Test that each School Champion takes), so you won't have the benefit of seeing the questions in writing. It is important to listen carefully. The moderator will read each question only once, and you want to be sure to hear all the clues that might help you answer correctly.

Second, be sure to listen to the entire question before answering. Don't assume that you know what is going to be asked. You have only one chance to respond. Once you say an answer out loud, it is very unlikely that you will have time to change it before the moderator responds.

Third, don't let difficult-sounding words intimidate or sidetrack you. If the moderator trips over the pronunciation, he or she should automatically repeat the entire question. If you think having a word spelled will help you, then ask the moderator to spell it out. Just be aware that you can interrupt the competition only two times to ask either to have a question repeated or a word spelled. This rule applies to the Preliminary Competition and to the Final Round at each level of the Bee.

Finally, always speak very clearly with your best pronunciation. Don't worry if microphones are present because they make you sound very cool and extra important!

Some Bee rounds involve questions from a single topic, such as cultural geography; others are a mix of many topics. The first few rounds usually offer a choice of two answers so that you have a 50-50 chance of answering correctly. This is to help you relax.

Gradually, the questions become more difficult as you progress from round to round and from one level to the next. After all, the Bee is a contest, and ultimately only one student can be the champion. But if you stay cool, use your study tips, and look for clues, you'll be surprised at how many questions you will be able to answer correctly.

The questions that follow are organized first by the level of the Bee in which they were used, and then by the round in which they appeared. Since the titles of rounds can change from year to year, and since the sample questions are taken from several different years, the titles listed here are only representative of what you might encounter. You may also notice that some questions could fit in more than one category. This overlap is just the nature of geography. The round titles will give you a general idea of the focus of the questions included in them. The first couple of questions in each round are followed by a discussion in italics that points out clues and reminds you of the study tips that will lead you to the correct answer (in bold type). For the remaining questions in the round you are on your own. You will find the answers starting on page 123.

As you go through the questions, jot down new terms, facts, and place-names. Keep your study tools handy so you can put questions in their geographic context. Try timing yourself to get practice in answering within the 15-second time limit (12 seconds for the national Final Round questions). Since the Bee is an oral competition, consider having someone read the questions to you. That will teach you to listen carefully for clues. Most of all, have fun!

SCHOOL-LEVEL PRELIMINARY ROUNDS

Round 1: General U.S. Geography

1. Mauna Loa is a volcano in which state—Hawaii or Washington?
From studying state profiles and geographic comparisons, you know that Mauna Loa is the highest point in Hawaii. Even if you don't remember this, the Hawaiian-sounding name is a big clue. You correctly answer **Hawaii.**

2. Which state has a climate suitable for growing citrus fruits—California or Maine?
You know that oranges and grapefruit are citrus fruits and that they grow in warm places. Since California's climate is definitely warmer and sunnier than Maine's you correctly answer **California.**

3. Which city is a port on the East Coast—Boston or Galveston?

4. Mount McKinley is the highest peak in which state—Alaska or Wisconsin?

5. Which region receives more precipitation—western Texas or western Oregon?

6. Which largely agricultural state is part of the Deep South—Indiana or Mississippi?

7. Cape Hatteras is part of which state—North Carolina or North Dakota?

8. Which city was originally established as a Spanish mission—Chicago or San Antonio?

9. Which city is located in a marine west coast climate—Seattle or Baltimore?

10. Lake Seminole forms part of the border between Georgia and which other state—Ohio or Florida?

Round 2: U.S. Physical Geography

1. Which state has areas that are prone to avalanches—Colorado or Kansas?
The word "avalanches" is the clue here. From studying geographic terms, you know they are moving masses of snow that occur in high mountains. From your physical maps you know that Colorado has lots of mountains, so you correctly answer **Colorado.**

2. Which state has a predominantly arid climate—Tennessee or New Mexico?
You know that "arid" means "dry" or "little rainfall." From studying physical maps and climate maps you know the Southwest of the United States is dry and mostly desert. So you correctly answer **New Mexico.**

3. Coral reefs are found off the coast of which state—Florida or Connecticut?

4. Which state has a broad coastal plain—California or Georgia?

5. Which state has large areas of permafrost—Oklahoma or Alaska?

6. All of Louisiana's rivers ultimately flow into which body of water—the Gulf of Mexico or the Gulf of California?

7. What is the only mid-Atlantic state not bordered by the ocean—Maryland or Pennsylvania?

8. The easternmost point of land in the contiguous United States lies in which state—Delaware or Maine?

9. Lake Itasca, the source of the Mississippi River, is in which state—Pennsylvania or Minnesota?

10. Cars race on the Bonneville Salt Flats in the Great Salt Lake Desert. These flats are in which state—Indiana or Utah?

11. Which has a longer coastline—South Carolina or California?

12. Which covers parts of Missouri and Arkansas—the Sacramento Valley or the Ozark Plateau?

Round 3: Geographic Comparisons in the United States

1. Which state has a larger Hispanic population in terms of numbers—California or Wisconsin?

You know that Hispanic people speak Spanish as their primary language. From keeping up with current events you know that most Hispanic people in the United States come into the country from Mexico, a country that borders California. From studying place-names you also know that many cities in California have Spanish names (San Francisco, San Diego, Los Angeles). So you correctly answer **California.**

2. Which city is located closer to sea level—Denver or Los Angeles?

You know that Denver's nickname is the Mile High City, plus from your mental maps you know that Denver is the capital of Colorado, a very mountainous state, whereas Los Angeles is a city on the Pacific Ocean. So you correctly answer **Los Angeles.**

3. The shorter growing season occurs in which state—Georgia or Wyoming?

4. Which state contains higher land elevations—Idaho or Alabama?

5. Which state has more Civil War battlefields—Virginia or Oregon?

6. Which river is farther west—the Potomac River or the Colorado River?

7. Which state has a smaller area—Delaware or Mississippi?

8. Which state produces more cattle—New Hampshire or Texas?

9. Which state receives more precipitation—Washington or Nevada?

10. Which region is less densely populated—the Great Lakes or the Great Basin?

Round 4: Cultural Geography

1. The samba, which was originally brought from Africa, is a dance that was adapted and is highly popular on which other continent?

From history class, movies, and television, you know that the major movement of people from Africa involved the slave trade to North and South America. Knowing that this dance is not wildly popular in the United States might be enough to make you answer South America. Or, you might recognize that the samba is associated with Latin America. Since South America makes up the largest portion of Latin America you correctly answer **South America.**

2. Spices such as cinnamon, cumin, chili, and turmeric have been used not only as flavoring but also as medicine in South Asia's largest country. Name this country.

From studying political regions in your atlases, you know that

South Asia is usually considered to include India, Pakistan, Bangladesh, Nepal, and Bhutan. A quick check of your mental map tells you which is the largest, so you correctly answer **India.**

3. Lederhosen, thick leather shorts with suspenders, are part of a local costume worn especially in the Bavarian Alps in what country?

4. In which European country did the Olympics begin?

5. Hanukkah, an annual celebration characterized by the lighting of candles for eight days, is celebrated by the followers of which religion?

6. What is the main language spoken in the countries of North Africa?

7. Tacos, enchiladas, and tortillas are dishes that are typically associated with which Latin American country?

8. With which continent is the term "Middle Ages" most closely associated?

9. Machu Picchu, site of an Inca city in the Andes, is in which present-day country?

10. After English, what language is most widely spoken in North America?

Round 5: Continents

1. Scientists believe that about 120 million years ago, South America began to break away from which other continent?
From learning about plate tectonics and from studying the shapes of continents and their positions in relationship to each other, you correctly answer **Africa.**

2. The North Atlantic current brings warm waters from the tropics to the west coast of which continent?
From studying physical maps you know that the North Atlantic is the area of that ocean that lies north of the Equator and that the entire west coast of Europe borders the North Atlantic, so you correctly answer **Europe.**

3. Which continent is crossed by every line of longitude?

4. The world's longest mountain chain is on which continent?

5. Which continent has the world's largest known oil reserves?

6. Most of the islands in the Caribbean Sea are considered part of which continent?

7. Angel Falls, the world's highest waterfall, is on which continent?

8. Which continent, after Antarctica, has the fewest number of people?

9. The Great Rift Valley extends through much of the eastern portion of which continent?

10. The Danube River flows through ten countries on which continent?

11. The Great Dividing Range and the Gibson Desert are part of which continent?

12. Which continent, covering nearly one-third of the Earth's land surface, was crossed by Marco Polo?

Round 6: Physical Geography

1. What is the term for a part of an ocean or sea that cuts far into the bordering landmass and may contain one or more bays?

From studying physical features on maps and using your geographical reference book to learn about physical features, you narrow your choices to two terms: bay and gulf. Since the word "bay" is used in the question, you eliminate it as a possibility and correctly answer **gulf.**

2. The study of the processes in the Earth's atmosphere that produce day-to-day weather is called what?

From studying the Earth's atmosphere in science class or from watching weather reports on the evening news you know that weather forecasters are called meteorologists and that what they study is called **meteorology.**

3. The Richter scale is commonly used to measure the magnitude of what natural hazard?

4. What is the term for the part of a continent that extends beyond the shoreline beneath relatively shallow seawater?

5. U-shaped and hanging valleys are both types of landforms created by the movement of what type of physical feature?

6. The sudden, rapid movement of snow and ice down a slope is known as what?

7. What term is used for the end of a river—where it enters a lake, a larger river, or an ocean?

8. What is the term that refers to the several large sections into which the lithosphere is broken?

9. What word from the Norwegian language is used for a narrow, steep-sided inlet of the sea that was carved by a glacier?

10. The molten rock that is ejected from a volcano and flows across Earth's surface is known as what?

11. Santa Ana and chinook are names of what kind of meteorological activity?

12. What is the term for the artificial lake created when a river is dammed?

Round 7: World Geography

1. The port of Rotterdam is built on the delta of which major European river?

This question requires thinking in layers. From studying major world cities, you know Rotterdam is in the Netherlands. Using your mental map, you know that the country lies in northwestern Europe along the Atlantic Ocean. Now use your mental map to picture major rivers that flow across this region of Europe into the Atlantic Ocean, and you correctly answer **Rhine River.**

2. The Vistula River and Bialowieza National Park—northern Europe's largest area of virgin forest and home to the European bison—are in which country?

Don't let the difficult-sounding Bialowieza scare you. Here is where you might want to ask the moderator to spell a word. The spelling and the pronunciation are clues to the country where it is located. But a bigger clue is the Vistula River. From studying country profiles and physical maps you know that the Vistula is the chief river in **Poland.**

3. What is the name of the tiny sea creature that lives in colonies and whose rocklike skeletal remains create reefs or ring-shaped islands called atolls?

4. Name the country that is Mexico's leading trading partner.

5. A chain of large freshwater and saltwater lakes runs through what geologically active valley in East Africa?

6. What is the most frequent natural hazard, brought on by the monsoons, that affects low-lying Bangladesh?

7. Which African river—a major source of hydroelectric power and the site of Victoria Falls—forms the southern border of Zambia?

8. Which island country in the Atlantic experiences volcanic activity *and* makes extensive use of geothermal power?

9. About half of the world's population depends on what staple as it principal food source?

10. Which mountainous country in Europe includes more than 2,000 scattered islands and has one of the largest merchant fleets in the world?

11. The largest hole in Earth's vital ozone layer is located over which continent?

12. The Aegean, Ionian, and Adriatic Seas are all part of what larger sea?

Tiebreaker Questions

1. The Tropic of Capricorn passes through the largest island in the Indian Ocean. Name this island.

*You know from studying lines of latitude that the Tropic of Capricorn is 23¹/₂° south of the Equator. From your mental maps you know that the Indian Ocean lies between Africa and Australia. Running down your list of the world's 10 largest islands, you correctly answer **Madagascar**.*

2. What is the term for a spherical model of the Earth?

3. Name Canada's largest island in area.

4. What do the letters N-A-T-O stand for?

5. The Ganges Plain extends across much of the northern portion of which country?

6. In 1697, Spain ceded control of what is now Haiti to what country?

SCHOOL-LEVEL FINAL ROUND

The questions in the Final Round are similar to those in the Preliminary Competition, except they are more difficult. The questions are not grouped into geographic categories. Instead, it is a good bet that each question will test your knowledge about a different geographic subject. The exception to this is the series of questions that pertains to a map, graph, or other visual aid.

Map Questions

To answer the questions below, you will have to use the map on the facing page. This round tests your ability to identify U.S. states by their shapes, to find certain physical features and regions, and to read a map key. During the Bee you will be given a few minutes to study the map before answering your question.

1. Name the least populous state on the Gulf of Mexico.
Here is where those blank outline maps you've been studying will really come in handy. From them you know to focus your attention on the coastal area between Florida and Texas. By comparing the symbols in the map key with the symbols on the states in this region, you correctly answer **Mississippi.**

2. Which New England state has more than six million people?

3. Name New York's most populous neighbor.

4. What is the most populous state on the Mississippi River?

5. Which mid-Atlantic state has fewer than one million people?

6. All of Kentucky's neighbors have more than two million people except which state?

7. Which state that borders California has a population of more than four million people?

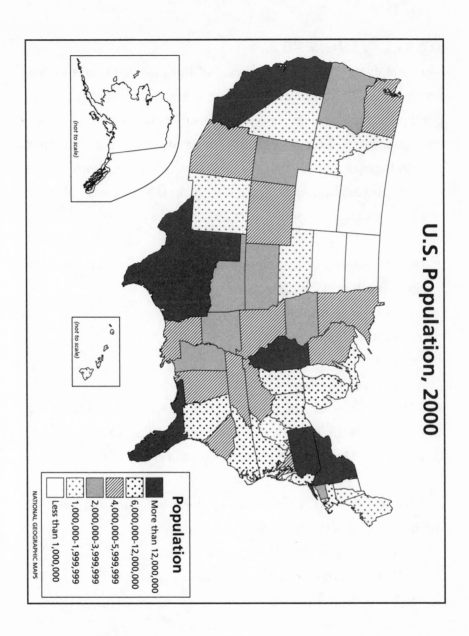

U.S. Population, 2000

(not to scale)

(not to scale)

Population

- More than 12,000,000
- 6,000,000–12,000,000
- 4,000,000–5,999,999
- 2,000,000–3,999,999
- 1,000,000–1,999,999
- Less than 1,000,000

NATIONAL GEOGRAPHIC MAPS

QUALIFYING TEST

The Qualifying Test is the only part of the Bee that is completely written. Its 70 questions, including a set pertaining to a map, graph, or other visual aid, cover a wide variety of geographic topics. Each question offers a choice of four answers, and you must choose the number (1, 2, 3, or 4) that you believe identifies the correct answer. Remember, the only time that you will take this test is if you are the winner of your School Bee.

1. The Olmec, one of Middle America's first civilizations, lived in a region bordering which body of water?

Gulf of California   1

Gulf of Mexico   2

Caribbean Sea   3

Chesapeake Bay   4

The Middle America clue narrows your choices to Caribbean Sea and Gulf of Mexico. You know that some of the earliest civilizations were in Mexico, so you correctly answer **2.**

2. What is the name of the Dutch explorer who, in 1642, became the first European to sight New Zealand?

Prince Henry the Navigator 1

James Cook   2

Ferdinand Magellan   3

Abel Tasman   4

From your mental maps of the area around New Zealand you know that the Tasman Sea separates New Zealand and Australia, so you correctly select Abel Tasman—4.

3. Which is the only Canadian province that borders the Great Lakes?

Quebec	1
Manitoba	2
Ontario	3
Alberta	4

4. The Kuznetsk Basin is an important industrial region in which country?

Germany	1
China	2
Canada	3
Russia	4

5. Which part of Asia is often referred to as a subcontinent, having its own continental plate?

China	1
India	2
Japan	3
Saudi Arabia	4

6. A New England saltbox, an English Tudor, and a Swiss chalet are all examples of what?

house	1
horse	2
boat	3
gun	4

7. In which state do the Jefferson, Madison, and Gallatin Rivers combine, forming the Missouri River?

Idaho	1
North Dakota	2
Montana	3
Colorado	4

8. Which capital city is located in the place that was once the center of the Aztec empire?

Lima	1
Mexico City	2
Buenos Aires	3
Brasília	4

Analogies

The Qualifying Test almost always has a series of analogies in which you are asked to compare two things that have something in common. For example, in the analogy "The peso is to Mexico as the WHAT is to Japan?" the answer is the yen because the yen is the currency of Japan, just as the peso is the currency in Mexico. See if you can figure out the following analogies.

9. Rhodesia is to Zimbabwe as WHAT is to Burkina Faso?

Malagasy Republic	1
Bechuanaland	2
French Somaliland	3
Upper Volta	4

From studying historical atlases and reading country profiles you know that Rhodesia is the former name of Zimbabwe. To complete the analogy, you must know the former name of Burkina Faso. The same sources that helped you with Rhodesia/Zimbabwe will lead you to choose Upper Volta—4.

10. Death Valley is to North America as Lake Assal is to WHAT?

Europe	1
South America	2
Africa	3
Australia	4

11. A square is to a United States city as a WHAT is to a South American city?

gazebo	1
villa	2
patio	3
plaza	4

Map Questions

Use the topographic map (opposite) to answer these three questions.

12. Which of the following points has the highest elevation?

A   1

B   2

C   3

D   4

From the contour line closest to point A, you know its elevation is 9,800 feet; point B is 10,050 feet (10,000 + 50 feet for the contour interval); point C is 9,500 feet; and point D is 9,807, so you select point B—2.

13. Which of the following is the approximate elevation of point F?

9,450 feet	1
9,610 feet	2
9,650 feet	3
9,700 feet	4

14. If you hike directly from point G to point D, which of the following describes your route?

First a gradual ascent, then a steep ascent   1

First a gradual descent, then a steep descent   2

First a gradual descent, then an increasing ascent 3

First a gradual ascent, then a steepening descent 4

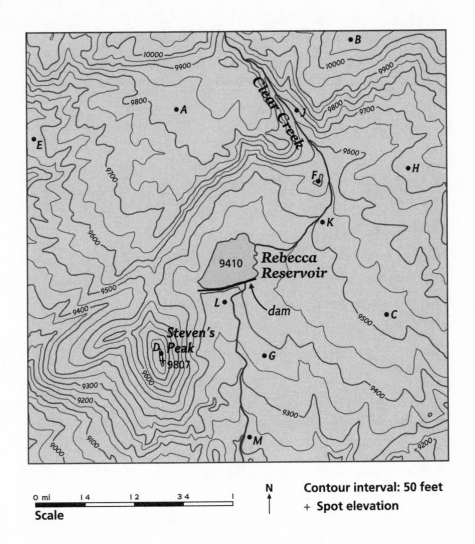

| 0 mi | 1 4 | 1 2 | 3 4 | 1 |

Scale

N
↑

Contour interval: 50 feet

+ Spot elevation

STATE-LEVEL PRELIMINARY ROUNDS

At the state level before the official questioning begins there is a warm-up round to help you relax. Your answers to these questions do not count. As with the school level, the first few rounds at the state offer a choice of answers.

Round 1: Cultural Geography

1. Which country has the world's largest Muslim population—Indonesia or Mexico?

If you have studied maps showing world religions you will know the answer immediately. If you haven't, you might reason that Mexico was settled by the Spanish, followers of Christianity not Islam. Either way, you correctly answer **Indonesia.**

2. Which country has more people who speak a Germanic language—Denmark or Azerbaijan?

From your mental political maps you know that Denmark is bordered by Germany on the south and that Azerbaijan borders Russia, so you correctly answer **Denmark.**

3. Cliff divers who plunge into the ocean are a popular tourist attraction in cities along the Pacific Ocean in which country—Mexico or Paraguay?

4. A 125-mile-long ice-skating race on frozen canals is a popular national event in which country—Portugal or the Netherlands?

5. Galileo worked in Pisa and Padua in which country—Italy or Poland?

6. Which city is claimed by both Israelis and Palestinians—Jerusalem or Amman?

7. Hindu worshipers cleanse their souls by bathing in the Ganges River in which country—Afghanistan or India?

8. The Chukchi are Arctic herders who live just west of the International Date Line in which country—Russia or Canada?

9. Which city in Africa is sometimes called the "city of a thousand minarets" because of the many Muslim prayer towers that mark its skyline—Cape Town or Cairo?

10. In which desert would you find the San, a nomadic group, using empty ostrich eggs as canteens for carrying water—the Kalahari or the Atacama?

Round 2: Physical Geography

1. In high mountain areas, rocks are often weathered by which process—frost action or wave refraction?
*The clue is "high mountain areas." You know that these places are far from the sea and therefore couldn't be weathered by waves. Plus such areas are cold, so you correctly answer **frost action.***

2. Which term describes a body of water that occasionally or seasonally dries up—intermittent or brackish?
*The words "occasionally" and "seasonally" suggest not continuous, so you correctly answer **intermittent**.*

3. Which type of map shows elevations above sea level—a topographic map or a cartogram?

4. Which type of tree is more common in boreal forests of the far north—deciduous trees or evergreen trees?

5. The parallel of latitude $66^{1/2}°$ south is known as what—the Tropic of Capricorn or the Antarctic Circle?

6. Granite is which type of rock—igneous or sedimentary?

7. What is the term for the boundary between two masses of air of differing temperatures—contact zone or front?

8. On average, which type of climate receives more rainfall in a year—a marine west coast climate or a steppe climate?

9. What term is used to describe a fracture in the Earth's crust—fault or slump?

10. What is the name for the part of Earth that includes all life forms—hydrosphere or biosphere?

Round 3: Cultural Geography

1. Which country, bordering Russia and Sweden, was settled by people who migrated from the region around the Volga River in the first century A.D.?
*Your mental political map should tell you immediately that only one country is bordered by both Russia and Sweden: **Finland.***

2. Name the most populous city on the Korean peninsula.
*Most often, but not always, the capital city of a country is its most populous city. You know from your political mental maps that the Korean peninsula is made up of North Korea and South Korea, but from your country profiles you know that South Korea has more people. So you correctly answer that country's capital, **Seoul.***

3. The name of Central America's smallest country in area means "the savior" in Spanish. Name this country.

4. Which mountain system in northwestern Africa was named for the legendary giant who is often shown carrying the Earth on his back?

5. The Bolshoi Theater, which is famous for its ballet performances, is a cultural attraction in what large country in the Eastern Hemisphere?

6. Confucianism developed and has been practiced for more than 2,000 years in which Asian country?

7. What landlocked country is named for the revolutionary leader who helped free much of northern South America from Spanish rule?

8. Place de la Concorde, the site where Marie-Antoinette, Louis XVI, and many others were guillotined during the 1790s, is located in which European capital city?

9. The Sistine Chapel, famous for Michelangelo's paintings on its ceiling, is a popular attraction in which very small European country?

10. Most of Argentina's citizens trace their ancestry to which continent?

Round 4: Economic Geography

1. The leading grain crop in Bangladesh is a staple food for the country's people. Name this grain.

From your political mental map you know that Bangladesh is in South Asia. You also know that rice is a principal food of most people in Asia, so you correctly answer **rice.**

2. Which Canadian province produces more than half of the country's manufactured goods?

Even if you haven't studied profiles of Canadian provinces, you know from your mental maps that Ontario borders all of the Great Lakes and has access to the St. Lawrence Seaway. This puts *it in a better position than any other Canadian province to import materials needed for manufacturing and to export finished goods. So you correctly answer **Ontario**.*

3. Years of rapid industrial growth around Kraków have left which eastern European country with severe environmental problems?

4. Name the economic activity that has become the chief source of income for most countries in the Caribbean.

5. Name the sea located between Norway and Great Britain that has major oil reserves.

6. What canal in Egypt allows ships to avoid the long trip around Africa?

7. More than half the world's desalination plant capacity is on what arid peninsula in Asia?

8. De Beers is a South African company that is the world's largest producer of what gemstone?

9. The world's second largest consumer of oil must import nearly all of its supply of that resource. Name this East Asian country.

10. Coffee is thought to have originated in the landlocked country that borders Somalia. Name this country.

Round 5: Current Events

The questions in this round assume that you are keeping up with events in the news. If you are, then there are abundant clues in the questions. If you aren't, then the only clues that you will find are references to a general location, as you will see from the following questions, all of which were asked in the 2001 State Preliminary Competition. Note: The use of italics for such words as "not," "peninsula," and "country" is for emphasis only.

1. In October 2000, terrorist suicide bombers in a small boat attacked the Navy destroyer U.S.S. *Cole* moored for refueling in a harbor in which Middle Eastern country?

2. A tanker loaded with chemicals sank in the English Channel off the coast of what country in October 2000?

3. The leaders of two neighboring countries on a peninsula in Asia met for the first time in a historic summit in June 2000. Name the *peninsula*.

4. Slobodan Milosevic was removed from office by a combination of democratic elections and popular revolution in which Balkan *country* in October 2000?

5. Which Scandinavian country chose *not* to adopt the euro, the common currency of the European Union, in a vote held in September 2000?

6. In December 2000, Ethiopia signed a peace accord ending a two-year border war with which country that was originally carved out of Ethiopia's territory?

7. An earthquake of 7.6 magnitude struck Central America in mid-January 2001, causing many deaths and massive mudslides in which country?

8. In May 2000, citizens of which European capital city made Ken Livingstone their first ever elected mayor?

9. In November 2000, the longest automobile tunnel in the world, linking the city of Bergen with its national capital, was opened by King Harald V of which *country?*

10. In mid-October 2000, an outbreak of the disease caused by the Ebola virus struck which nation on the northern shore of Lake Victoria?

Round 6: Historical Geography

1. The Central Powers, an alliance that included Germany, Austria-Hungary, Bulgaria, and the Ottoman Empire, fought together during which major European conflict?

The clue "major European conflict" leads you to think of a world war. From history books and studying historical maps, you know that Austria-Hungary and the Ottoman Empire no longer existed at the time of World War II, so you correctly answer **World War I.**

2. To visit the ruins of Persepolis, an ancient ceremonial capital of Persia, you would have to travel to what present-day country? *From history books or from studying country profiles, you know that Persia is the former name of Iran, so you correctly answer* **Iran.**

3. The Oyo Empire of the Yoruba tribe was located north of present-day Lagos in which African country?

4. Name the vast, mineral-rich region east of the Urals that was conquered in part by the Cossacks for Ivan the Terrible?

5. Two large countries in southern Africa achieved independence from Portugal in 1975. Name *one* of them.

6. What Bavarian city, located on the Pegnitz River, was the scene of Allied trials of German war criminals after World War II?

7. During the 1961 Bay of Pigs invasion, exiles from which Caribbean country tried unsuccessfully to overthrow their country's government?

8. The ancient town of Beersheba has long been a source of water and a trade center for Bedouins traveling in the Negev. Beersheba is in which present-day country?

9. Cappadocia, an ancient region north of the Taurus Mountains in Asia Minor, is located in which present-day country?

10. U.S. troops fought Muslim groups in the Moro Wars of 1901 to 1913 on Mindanao and other islands in which present-day country?

Round 7: Political Geography

1. Name *one* of the two South American countries that have territorial claims in Antarctica.

If you have studied a political map of Antarctica, this will be an easy question. If you haven't, then a check of your mental map of the world shows you that Chile and Argentina are the two South American countries closest to Antarctica, which makes them a jumping-off point for expeditions to that continent and makes them the most likely of all the South American countries to hold claims on Antarctica. Since you have to name only one, answer either **Argentina** *or* **Chile.**

2. The large Danish island of Kalaallit Nunaat, which borders the Arctic and Atlantic Oceans, is more commonly known by what name?

A check of your mental map of the world and of the list of 10 largest islands reveals that there is only one large island that borders both the Arctic and Atlantic Oceans. Even if you don't know that it belongs to Denmark, you know the answer must be **Greenland.**

3. The former territories of Tanganyika and Zanzibar united to form what country in 1964?

4. The no-fly zone over northern Iraq is designed to protect what ethnic minority group?

5. Montevideo and what other national capital city are located on the Río de la Plata?

6. Name the large island in the eastern Mediterranean that is politically divided between people of Greek and Turkish heritage.

7. Grenada, southernmost of the Windward Islands, is also part of what larger chain of islands?

8. The Oder and Neisse Rivers serve as the boundary between Germany and which eastern European country?

9. A narrow strip of Malaysia separates the two parts of what small country on the island of Borneo?

10. Most of the islands in the Aegean Sea are part of what country?

Tiebreaker Questions
1. Name the country that controls the straits that connect the Mediterranean and Black Seas.
From your mental physical maps you know that these straits are at the eastern end of the Mediterranean Sea. A check of your mental political maps of the region shows you that there is only one country that borders both the Black Sea and the Mediterranean

Sea and that also lies on both sides of these straits. Reasoning that this country would control the straits, you correctly answer **Turkey.**

2. The capital of Belarus is also the administrative headquarters of the Commonwealth of Independent States. Name this city.

3. Although traditionally famous for its beef, which South American country has rapidly increased its dairy industry in provinces along the Paraná River?

4. The Islamic university in Fès is one of the oldest universities in the world. This institution is located in which North African country?

5. What kind of structure, used for transporting water over long distances, was first built in Mesopotamia but later was perfected by engineers of the Roman Empire?

6. The ridge of what mountain range creates the continental divide in northern Mexico?

STATE-LEVEL FINAL ROUND

The only rounds of questions organized by topics in the State Finals are those that deal with maps, graphs, photographs, or some other visual material. The following randomly selected examples are designed to give you an idea of what you can expect for these kinds of rounds.

Immigration Graph

This graph shows the number of legal immigrants coming into the United States from Europe, North America, Asia, South America, and Africa from 1900 through the 1990s. You must use the graph to answer the questions on the facing page.

IMMIGRANTS ENTERING THE UNITED STATES

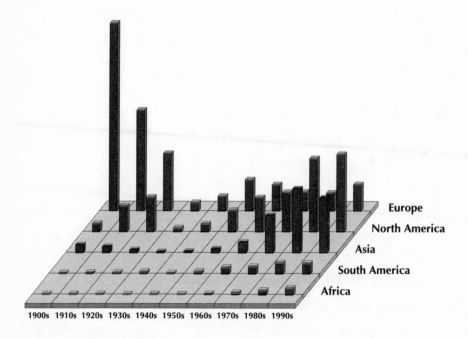

1. Since 1900, which continent has been the source of the fewest immigrants arriving in the United States?
Looking at the graph, you can see that the bars in the first line across the bottom are the shortest on the graph. By looking along the right side of the graph you can find the continent that this line represents. Putting the two bits of information together, you correctly answer **Africa.**

2. During which two decades was the total number of immigrants entering the United States the lowest?

3. Which continent was the only one to show an increase from the 1920s to the 1930s?

4. Name the first decade that Europe was not the leading source of immigrants to the United States.

5. Two continents experienced *their* highest immigration to the United States in the 1990s. Name *one* of them.

6. Which continent experienced a significant increase in the number of immigrants from the 1950s until the 1990s, when a slight drop-off occurred?

7. Since the 1970s, which continent has been the source of the greatest number of immigrants entering the United States?

Photo Questions

1. Name this city in Europe.

Europe limits the field, but the real clue is the Eiffel Tower, which rises above the city. If you can identify this landmark, you know immediately that the correct answer is **Paris.**

2. This gold funeral mask is of an ancient king of Mycenae, a city that gave its name to an ancient Aegean civilization. The Mycenaean civilization was centered in what present-day country?

.

3. Camels wait to be loaded with blocks of the mineral being pried loose from a dry lake bed in the Danakil Depression. Name this mineral, which has been a mainstay of North Africa's caravan trade for centuries.

4. Name this mountain peak on the boundary between Switzerland and Italy.

Map Questions

This round requires two answers to each question. Each question provides information about a chief export of a country that is numbered on the map of Africa. You must identify the country by its number *and* by its name. You must answer *both* parts correctly to receive credit for each question.

1. A country in West Africa that was once known for its ivory trade is now the world's leading exporter of cacao. What is the number and name of this country?

The West Africa regional clue limits the numbers to 6, 7, 9, 10, 12, and 13. Checking your mental political map of Africa, you recognize 12 as Côte d'Ivoire (French for Ivory Coast), a country whose name obviously has some link to the ivory trade, so you correctly answer **12, Côte d'Ivoire.**

2. The country once known as Southern Rhodesia is Africa's leading exporter of tobacco. What is the number and name of this country?

3. A country known for its many unique species of plants and animals is also one of the world's chief sources of natural vanilla and graphite. What is the number and name of this country?

4. Africa's leading exporter of olive oil is bordered by the Mediterranean Sea and two of the continent's leading oil producers. What is the number and name of this country?

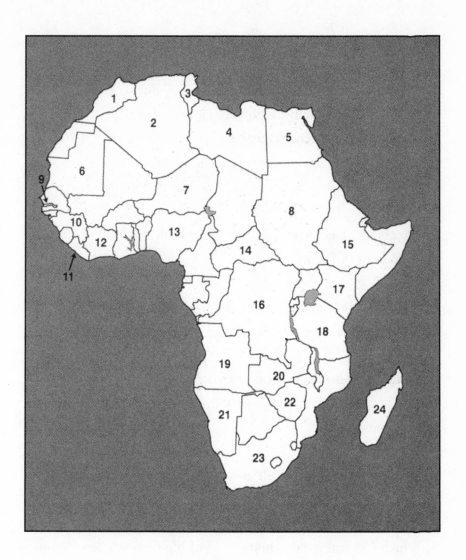

Note: The questions for this map round were used
in the 1993 Bee and were accurate at that time.

NATIONAL-LEVEL PRELIMINARY ROUNDS

The following questions represent the types of questions and geographic categories that you can expect during the nonvisual rounds of the National Preliminary Competition.

Round 1: World Geography

1. The Gulf of Aden lies between the Horn of Africa and what peninsula?

2. Which Baltic country is bordered by both the Gulf of Finland and the Gulf of Riga?

3. What country on the Gulf of Honduras was formerly known as British Honduras?

Round 2: Economic Geography

1. Broken Hill, Mount Isa, and Kalgoorlie are mining centers in what country?

2. Malawi depends on which country bordering the Indian Ocean for rail access to the sea?

3. Which Central Asian country east of the Caspian Sea contains enormous, untapped fossil fuel reserves along its western border?

Round 3: Cultural Geography

1. People who speak Cushitic languages live primarily in the eastern part of which continent?

2. The Hmong people have traditionally lived in the mountainous regions of Thailand, Laos, Vietnam, and which neighboring country?

3. Most people in Sri Lanka are followers of a religion that developed as a reaction to certain elements of Hinduism. Name this religion.

Round 4: General Geography

1. Place these three major cities in order according to their latitude, from north to south: Manila, Beijing, Taipei.

2. Place these rivers in order according to their length, from longest to shortest: Danube, Elbe, Volga.

3. Which of the following countries does not lie on the prime meridian: Spain, Burkina Faso, or Cameroon?

Round 5: Physical Geography

1. "Terminal" and "recessional" describe two types of a feature formed by the glacial deposition of soil, rocks, and other material. What is the term for this feature?

2. In the early 20th century, a scientist devised a climate classification system based on vegetation regions, temperature, and rainfall that is commonly used today. Identify the scientist for whom the classification system is named.

3. What is the term for a seamount with a completely flat top?

CHAPTER **5**

Tips from Bee Finalists

This chapter provides advice from previous school, state, and national champions about when to get involved, what to study, and how to relax. Although many of the contributors are now in high school or college, at one time or another they were all Bee kids just like you. So listen up!

• •

Try to get involved in the school Bees in the fourth grade or as soon as possible. The first couple of years, the competition will be challenging, even discouraging, and not as easy as it looks. You have to put a lot of time and effort into studying geography to really do well. I can't exactly pinpoint just what it is that I like so much about geography, but it is not in any way tedious studying for the Bee.

Erik Bolt, 2001 State Bee Champion, Homeschooler, South Bend, Indiana (8th Grade)

•••••••••••••••••••••••••••

I believe that what helped me prepare for the Bee the most was my love for reading. By reading lots of books, magazines, and especially newspapers, you can gain a vast knowledge of other places and cultures. During the actual Bee, I think the best things to do are listen carefully to the whole question, use the given time to really think about your answer, and be confident when you give your answer.
Rachel Schuerger, 2001 State Bee Champion, Alaska (8th Grade)

•••••••••••••••••••••••••••

The Geographic Bee is a great experience. While competing, try to remember as much as you can, but remember, winning the Bee isn't everything. So long as you achieve your personal goal, then you are still a winner.
Seyi Fayanju, 1994 and 1996 State Bee Champion, New Jersey, and 1996 National Champion (7th Grade)

•••••••••••••••••••••••••••

The first time I competed in the Bee was when I was in fourth grade, and I tied for third place at the school level. In the fifth grade, I was eighth in South Carolina, but in my sixth-grade year I lost in the preliminary state rounds. I competed in the national preliminaries in the seventh grade. Finally, in the last year that I was eligible to participate I won the National Championship. It just shows that it pays to keep trying!
David Beihl, 1998 and 1999 State Bee Champion, South Carolina, and 1999 National Champion (8th Grade)

••••••••••••••••••••••••••

Try to see the Bee as a game rather than as an evaluation of your ability or intelligence. Realize that the same general areas of geography are covered at all levels of the Bee. This can help you plan what to study. Don't cram. Study a little every day. Don't let the pressure get to you. Just do your best and have fun.

Susannah Batko-Yovino, 1990 State Bee Champion, Pennsylvania, and National Champion (6th Grade)

••••••••••••••••••••••••••

To prepare for the Geographic Bee, I have studied atlases, other geographic reference books, played geography board games, and used software such as the National Geographic GeoBee program. It's important not to get too flustered when you don't remember the answer to a question right away. Try to think it through before giving your answer.

Mattias Gassman, 2001 State Bee Finalist, Iowa (6th Grade)

••••••••••••••••••••••••••

Use your computer to play geography games. Use different kinds of atlases. They are best for studying maps, country information, and world figures and statistics. You will find information on things like currents, volcanoes, the shifting of continents, climate, the atmosphere, population, and much more.

Jabari Ritchie, 1997 State Bee Finalist, Belle Vue Middle School, Tallahassee, Florida (8th Grade)

••••••••••••••••••••••••••

Geography pops up in the news, magazine articles, history books, and science class—practically everywhere. Geography is not the dull and rather pointless memorization of places, but rather the study of how the land affects the people in it. So get your head out of the atlas and start reading!

Michael Oh, 2001 State Bee Champion, New York (8th Grade)

••••••••••••••••••••••••••

Here's how I study: I frequently look at the National Geographic Web site and do the sample Bee questions. I like to read the articles in NATIONAL GEOGRAPHIC magazine and *Faces* magazine. I try to watch the national news every evening, and I like to look at the atlas I won at the Wisconsin State Bee last year.

How do I deal with being afraid at the Bee? I try to remember how much I like geography questions and just take them one at a time. I try to remember that the Geographic Bee is a fun competition and to see just how far I can go!

Sean Rao, 2001 State Bee Champion, Wisconsin (6th Grade)

••••••••••••••••••••••••••

My advice to any Geographic Bee participant is to read all the books you can about science, geography, and history. It also helps to keep up on current events. One good way to remember important stories is to cut them out of the paper and paste them in a notebook.

John Rice, 2000 State Bee Champion, North Dakota (6th Grade)

●●●●●●●●●●●●●●●●●●●●●●●●●●●

Stay calm! Take the full time and think over the question carefully. It definitely doesn't help to answer as fast as you can. You can't possibly learn everything about geography, so structure your studying in some way. I started out by going over maps of all the continents, first just learning all the major things (e.g., biggest mountains and mountain ranges, capital cities, biggest and most important waterways, peninsulas, isthmuses, gulfs, etc.), and then learning the more intricate things (e.g., big cities and rivers that run through those cities, capes, bays, etc.). All the while couple this with cultural, historical, and political facts. Experiment and do what works best for you, but be careful not to get lost. Geography is a big subject!

Get your hands on anything and everything that has to do with the world. You can never have too much material to study. You are about to embark on a journey that can take you around the world, if you let it. One Bee can lead to the next, and who knows where you'll end up. So, good luck and enjoy yourself!

Nicholas Jachowski, 2001 State Bee Champion, Hawaii
(8th Grade)

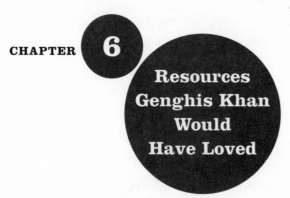

CHAPTER **6**

Resources
Genghis Khan
Would
Have Loved

Many centuries ago the great Mongol ruler, Genghis Khan, united his nomad tribes into a formidable army. His Golden Horde swept across the Central Asian steppe on horseback, terrorizing and plundering settlements from the Caspian Sea to the Pacific Ocean. They devastated cities, redirected rivers, and left deserts crowded with fleeing refugees. The Chinese built the Great Wall to keep the "barbarians" out, the Persians hid from them, and the Europeans fell like matchsticks. At the time of Genghis Khan's death in 1227, he controlled one of the greatest land empires the world has ever known.

Mr. Khan succeeded because, unlike the Europeans, his army did not wear heavy armor or burden itself with supply wagons that could break down. The Mongols traveled exceptionally light and fast. Their excellent use of geographic information made this possible. Mongol scouts went out months ahead of the main army, secretly gathering crucial information about terrain, vegetation, and settlements. This later assured the best routes, food for the men and ponies, and great hideaways. In a nutshell (or saddlebag), the Mongol scouts were simply the best.

Although great in the 13th century, Genghis's information was meager compared with what our current atlases, globes, and reference books can provide. Throw in television, the Internet, e-mail, and cell phones that allow instant information to flow around the globe, and you have an advantage that might have turned back even the Golden Horde.

The Mongols aside, just imagine how historic news headlines might have read if our current geographic information and communications technology had been available long ago. We might have seen: "GPS Navigation Guides Columbus to New World (film and details at 11:00)!" "Paul Revere E-Mails Alert from North Church!" "Custer's Lieutenant Faxes Map of Indian Camps." "Cell Phone Saves Captain Scott at South Pole."

The good news today is that for modest barter or a quick crusade to your local library, even ordinary peasants can obtain geographic learning materials the great Khan would have loved (and probably even killed for). An exhaustive list would make a book in itself, so this one simply highlights proven resources that will help you learn to think like a geographer.

ATLASES

Even if you're not scheming to plunder European villages, a good world atlas belongs in every ger, or yurt. This is the standard reference for Bee preparation and should include a full set of political, physical, and thematic maps (population, economic, climate, etc.). Also, look for country profiles, information about the oceans, plate tectonics, time zones, geographic comparisons, etc.

Our rapidly changing world alters the political landscape very quickly, so beware that if your atlas is more than five years old, some country names and boundaries may be outdated. The same is true for population figures and similar statistics. The rule of thumb is always to look for the most recent edition. Also, check to see if a less expensive paperback edition is available.

Large World Atlases

National Geographic Atlas of the World, 7th Edition,
National Geographic Society, Washington, D.C., 1999.
A superb collection of political, physical, urban, regional, and ocean-floor maps; thematic maps covering topics such as climate patterns, plate tectonics, population, economic trends, and world cultures; country profiles; satellite imagery; temperature and rainfall; geographic comparisons; and a comprehensive index.

The Times Atlas of the World: Comprehensive Edition,
10th Edition, Crown Publishing Group, New York, N.Y., 1999.
Emphasizes physical maps, with comprehensive coverage of every world region; thematic maps covering topics such as earthquakes, oceans, land cover, population, and energy; includes statistical information on countries and states and a complete index of place-names.

The Times of London Concise Atlas of the World, 8th Edition, Crown Publishing Group, New York, N.Y., 2001.

First-rate satellite images and maps of the continents; country profiles; and thematic maps, covering earthquakes, volcanoes, the oceans, climate, land cover, population, urbanization, minerals, communications, etc.

Midsize World Atlases

National Geographic Family Reference Atlas of the World, National Geographic Society, Washington, D.C., 2002.

A comprehensive, family-friendly atlas with sections about the world, continents, oceans, and space. It includes an expansive thematic section with maps, graphs, charts, photographs, and insightful text for each topic, an extensive list of geographic comparisons, and an index of more than 75,000 place-names.

Rand McNally Goode's World Atlas, 20th Edition, Rand McNally & Co., Skokie, Ill., 2000.

A comprehensive world atlas that includes a wide variety of thematic maps; world and regional maps; geographic comparison tables; and explanations of map scale, map projections, and Earth-Sun relationships.

Hammond World Atlas, 3rd Edition, Hammond World Atlas Corp., Union, N.J., 2000.

Satellite imagery; terra-scape maps of land and ocean floor terrain; thematic maps and graphs on population, living standards, agriculture and manufacturing, climate, and the environment. A Quick Reference Guide and city maps are also included.

Children's and Student World Atlases

National Geographic Student Atlas of the World,
National Geographic Society, Washington, D.C., 2001. (Grades 6–10)
Packed with informative thematic maps that explore the world's physical and human systems, focusing on geology, climate, vegetation, population, economies, food, energy, and mineral resources. For each continent there are three sets of maps (physical and political, climate and precipitation, population and predominant economies) plus a photo essay. The atlas clearly explains map types and how to read them and includes Web sites for finding further information and updating statistics.

National Geographic World Atlas for Young Explorers Revised and Expanded Edition, National Geographic Society,
Washington, D.C., 2003. (Grades 3–7)
Winner of the *Parents' Choice* Gold Award, this atlas contains world thematic maps, photo essays, satellite images, physical and political maps of each continent, country profiles, geographic comparisons, a glossary, and a comprehensive index.

Children's Millennium Atlas of the World,
Rand McNally & Company, Skokie, Ill., 1999. (Grades 4–8)
Illustrated geographic information and numerous physical, political, and thematic maps of the world, continents, and regional areas.

Maps.com World Reference Atlas (iPowered),
Maps.com, Santa Barbara, Calif., 2001. (Grades 6–12)
Excellent thematic and political maps that illustrate the dynamic effect people have on the globe. Designed to be colorful, easy-to-read, and informative for the younger reader.

Student Atlas of World Geography, 2nd Edition, John L. Allen.
McGraw Hill Higher Education, Burr Ridge, Ill., 2000. (College)
Full-color maps and data sets provide a clear picture of the recent economic, political, and environmental demographic changes in every world region.

Specialty Atlases

National Geographic Atlas of the Ocean, Sylvia A. Earle.
National Geographic Society, Washington, D.C., 2001.
Features more than 150 detailed maps, photographs, and state-of-the art satellite images, charting every aspect of the ocean world. Includes details about climate, weather, currents, tides, and the ocean's living systems as well as essays by experts on topics ranging from deep-sea drilling to predicting El Niño.

National Geographic Atlas of World History, Noel Grove.
National Geographic Society, Washington, D.C., 1997.
Traces world history from the dawn of humans to the 21st century; hundreds of maps, photographs, and historic paintings; includes fact boxes, biographies, time lines, chronology of major wars, lists of Popes and the rulers of the British and Roman Empires, etc.

National Geographic United States Atlas for Young Explorers Updated Edition, National Geographic Society, Washington, D.C., 2004. (Grades 3–7)

Superb U.S., state, and regional maps explain the primary geographical relationships in the United States. Includes concise state profiles, photographic essays on each region, and thematic spreads on topics such as territorial growth, the natural environment, population, and endangered species.

World Bank Atlas 2001, 33rd Edition, World Bank, Washington, D.C., 2001.

Easy-to-read world maps, tables, and graphs highlight key social, economic, and environmental data for the world's economies. Topics include infant mortality, gross domestic product, female labor, drinking water, forest cover, and CO_2 emissions.

The Atlas of World Religions, Anita Ganeri and Paola Ravaglia. McGraw Hill Childrens, Columbus, Ohio, 2001.

This heavily illustrated, large-format book reviews the religions of the world, highlighting key religious practices and holy sites.

Rand McNally Children's Atlas of World Wildlife, Elizabeth G. Fagan and Jan Wills. Rand McNally, Skokie, Ill., 1993.

Introduces the animals of the world and their habitats. Arranged by geographical area, each section shows how various species live and interact within their environments through colorful maps, photographs, and illustrations.

Magellan Geographix World History Atlas, Maps.com,
Santa Barbara, Calif. 2000.
A collection of clear, attractive, and easy-to-read historical maps.
Comprehensive global coverage of major historical periods.

Student Atlas of World Politics, 4th Edition, John L. Allen.
McGraw Hill Higher Education, Burr Ridge, Ill., 1999.
Emphasizes current affairs that reflect recent developments in
political geography and international relations. This collection of
maps and data is particularly useful for exploring the relationships
between geography and world politics.

Dushkin Student Atlas of Economic Development, John L. Allen.
McGraw Hill Higher Education, Burr Ridge, Ill. 1997.
Provides a unique combination of maps and data to explore the
recent agricultural, industrial, demographic, and environmental
changes that affect economic development around the world.

GEOGRAPHIC REFERENCE BOOKS
The National Geographic Desk Reference,
National Geographic Society, Washington, D.C., 1999.
A world of geography distilled into a single volume. Succinct and
accurate information on all the essential geographic topics, with
great maps, charts, and photographs.

Exploring Your World: The Adventure of Geography,
National Geographic Society, Washington, D.C., 1989.

Covers in dictionary format the same topics found in the above-mentioned Desk Reference but in simpler terms. This volume is out of print, but it's worth finding in the library or used-book store.

Webster's Geographical Dictionary, Third Edition.
Merriam-Webster, Inc., Springfield, Mass., 1997.
Provides an alphabetical listing of more than 48,000 places and features, with concise information about each plus hundreds of maps and tables.

Geographica's World Reference, Laurel Glen Publishing, San Diego, Calif., 2000.
Concise information divided into three comprehensive parts: Planet Earth, People and Society, and A–Z Country Listings. Many illustrations and an excellent gazetteer.

The Handy Geography Answer Book, Matthew Todd Rosenberg. Visible Ink Press, Canton, Ohio, 1999.
An easy-to-use book that explains 1,000 of the most intriguing geography questions that apply to today's world. Also includes an extensive geographic comparison section.

ALMANACS

The World Almanac for Kids 2002, Elaine Israel.
World Almanac Books, Mahwah, N.J., 2001.
Abundant information on essential topics, such as animals, computers, inventions, movies and television, religion, and sports.

This factbook includes many photographs, illustrations, and maps, along with puzzles, brainteasers, and other activities.

The Scholastic Kid's Almanac for the 21st Century,
Elaine Pascoe, Deborah Kops, Bob Italiano, and David C. Bell.
Scholastic, Inc., New York, N.Y., 1999.
Rich with graphics and facts every schoolkid should know in a straightforward yet creative text.

The World Almanac and Book of Facts 2002, Ken Park.
World Almanac Books, New York, N.Y., 2001.
A classic annual with a price that drops during the year. Crammed with global facts from farm imports to volcanic activity to baseball batting averages.

GEOGRAPHY TEXTBOOKS

Fourth through eighth grade social studies textbooks are a great source for learning about geography. As your skills improve, check out the textbooks for more advanced levels. Don't be afraid of college textbooks. Although they are more difficult to read, if you understand geography fundamentals, they offer a comprehensive and advanced tutorial on most topics. You can find these texts in bookstores, especially college and secondhand bookstores. Or surf the Internet for the best bargains (search under "used college textbooks"). College and university libraries shelve textbooks. Many state and community colleges will allow you to obtain a library card so you can borrow books.

LITERATURE

Reading nonfiction books on just about any topic—exploration, sports, survival, wars, biography, even regional cookbooks!—can help expand your geographic knowledge. Even fiction has to have a setting, and most authors carefully research the background for their plots. This means that just about anything you read can add to your geographic knowledge.

CYBERSPACE RESOURCES

There are great stops on our rapidly emerging information super-highway. Beware that URL addresses change frequently. If you have trouble finding any, consult one of the popular Internet search engines, such as Google (www.google.com) or Lycos (www.lycos.com), and simply request the site name.

National Geographic Society: www.nationalgeographic.com
Chockfull of information on geography initiatives at the Society and lots of stuff for kids.

GeoBee Challenge: www.nationalgeographic.com/geobee/
Provides five new National Geographic Bee questions each day.

Quintessential Instructional Archive: www.quia.com/dir/geo
Good flash card quiz site, with plenty of other interactive games.

Carmen Sandiego: www.carmensandiego.com
This great quiz game tests your geographic knowledge.

About Geography: www.geography.about.com
This site offers free downloads and links to other geography sites, outline maps, and current events.

Population Reference Bureau: www.prb.org
The best source for world population, with interactive population pyramids, a quiz, recent news, country data, and links to other sites.

The CIA World Factbook: www.cia.gov/cia/publications/factbook/
Maps, current information, and background data on every country.

NASA on the Web: www.earth.nasa.gov
Click For Kids Only. This site explores air, water, land, and hazards at a level useful for Bee contestants.

United Nations: www.un.org
Full of country facts, statistics, current events, maps, and more.

The Journalist's Toolbox: www.journaliststoolbox.com
Features 7,000 links to all of the world's on-line newspapers and other sources of information. A great source for current events from a global perspective.

Environment Canada: www.cws-scf.ec.gc.ca
Click on Kids Zone for numerous links to educational resources and games.

GEOsources: The Canadian Geography Web site: www.ccge.org
Canada's top site to learn about its people and places. Offers news
and quizzes.

National Atlas of Canada: www.atlas.gc.ca
Great technical information, maps, and educational materials.

GREAT GEO GAMES

GeoBee, National Geographic Society, Washington, D.C.
A CD-ROM game that allows as many as four students at a time
to test and improve their knowledge of world geography by
answering questions used in the National Geographic Bee.

GeoBee Challenge, National Geographic Society
(available August 2002 at Target stores)
A board game in which players compete to gather Golden Geo
Awards by correctly answering questions based on those used in
the National Geographic Bee and the *GeoBee* CD-ROM.

Name That State Game, Educational Insights,
Rancho Dominguez, Calif.
An entertaining board game that teaches locations, capital cities,
and scenic features for all 50 states.

Name That Country Game, Educational Insights
A board game that uses names, salutations, or special features on

postcards to help you identify countries and capitals. The game can be played at varying levels of difficulty and tests knowledge of rivers, major cities, languages, and currencies.

Go Travel: Africa, Travel by Games, Clinton, Iowa
A fun card game that tests your knowledge of history, geography, people, plants, animals, and problems of Africa.

GeoSafari Game of the States, Educational Insights
Hop in the car for a fun-filled trip around the United States. Players work their way around the country by answering questions about each state from 99 GeoSafari question cards.

GeoSafari Talking Globe, Educational Insights
A talking geography quiz game and globe all in one. The 5,000 interactive-question database challenges players about their world knowledge.

OTHER STUDY AIDS
Globes
Globes are available from a variety of manufacturers. Those produced by National Geographic can be found by visiting the Society's Web site (www.nationalgeographic.com) or calling 1-800-NGS-LINE/647-5463. As a general rule, the higher the price, the higher the quality and detail. Be sure to check the date of the product before ordering.

Magazines

NATIONAL GEOGRAPHIC magazine (also available on CD-ROM), National Geographic WORLD, *National Geographic for Kids!*, *Canadian Geographic, Time for Kids* (TFK), and newsweeklies, such as *Time, Newsweek,* and *U.S. News & World Report*, are packed with geographic information and include great maps, graphs, and pictures.

Television

Don't ignore this medium. Programming on Public Television (National Geographic Specials, *Nature, Bill Nye the Science Guy, Kratts' Creatures*, etc.), the brand new National Geographic Channel, CNN, C-SPAN, the Discovery Channel, the History Channel, and nightly news broadcasts will greatly expand your world.

Blank Outline Maps

Free downloads are available from

The NGS Map Machine: www.nationalgeographic.com

About Geography: www.geography.about.com

Outline Maps of Canada: www.canadainfolink.ca/blankmap.htm

If you don't have access to on-line resources, call US Map and Book Company, 1-800-458-2306.

Note to Teachers

The National Geographic Society developed the National Geographic Bee in response to concern about the lack of geographic knowledge among young people in the United States. In a ten-country Gallup survey conducted for the Society in 1988 and 1989, Americans 18 to 24 (the youngest group surveyed) scored lower than their counterparts in the other countries. Shocked by these results, the National Geographic Society spearheaded a campaign to return geography to American classrooms. Since 1989, the Bee has been one of several projects designed to encourage the teaching and study of geography. Just as important, the Bee makes learning geography fun. With nearly five million fourth through eighth graders entering each year, the Bee is now one of the nation's most popular academic contests.

Some parents and even a few teachers think the Bee might resemble an orderly Trivial Pursuit contest. Yet, in more than a decade of coordinating the California State Bee, I have not seen a single adult who arrives with that opinion leave with it intact.

Indeed, kids who correctly answer questions on glacial erosion, Hinduism, location, and changing political blocs humble a new flock of adults every year. The annual assembly of teachers, parents, and media is impressed not just with what the contestants know right off the bat, but with how they methodically answer questions that at first appear to stump them. This ability to think like a geographer—to integrate physical, cultural, and economic knowledge—shines through at every level of the Bee.

You may know that the Goals 2000: The Educate America Act, passed by Congress in 1994, included geography as one of nine core subjects. In the previous 50 years geography had slipped out of many schools as school days were shortened, funding declined, and other subjects elbowed into the curriculum. Since 1990, new initiatives and classroom activities are returning geography to America's classrooms. Among these the most important are training teachers in geography content and teaching methods, the adoption of the National Geography Standards, and the emergence of a Geographic Alliance Network to support teachers.

The National Geography Standards are an effective road map for teaching geography and for guiding interdisciplinary efforts across the curriculum. The standards emerged from a cooperative effort of the National Geographic Society, higher education, K-12 teachers, and professional associations. Many states have adopted part or all of these standards into their curriculum frameworks.

To interpret the standards for states and teachers, the National Geographic Society recently released *Path Toward World Literacy: A Standards-Based Guide to K–12 Geography.* This guide contains broad learning objectives and sample learning activities that are based upon six essential elements. It provides explanations and activities that assist teachers, curriculum writers, parents, and the general public to effectively integrate the geography standards into the school curriculum at all grade levels.

Although these efforts establish a framework for teaching geography, the Geographic Alliance Network prepares and supports teachers in the classroom. During the 1990s, the Society funded the creation of many state alliances to promote geographic education and awareness among teachers, students, and the public through:

- Professional growth seminars for teachers and student teachers, including school-site workshops, summer institutes, district in-service training, field trips, and teaching-methods classes
- University–K/12 Student Cooperation, including field trips, tutoring, presentations, and classroom support
- Developing and distributing educational materials, such as atlases, thematic maps, literature, map skills packets, and classroom lessons
- Promoting geography awareness and literacy among the public through newspaper inserts, editorials, national park handouts, Geobowls, Geography in Action, family geography nights, Web sites, etc.
- Supporting changes at local and state levels that promote geography across the curriculum

Teacher Consultants with specialized training in geographic education are the heart of every alliance. They can guide you toward the many resources available to make geography come alive in your classroom. In addition to this network, many state and county offices of education, universities, and individual school district initiatives offer geography resources, often in cooperation with the alliances.

Contact information for Bee registration, obtaining the *Path Toward World Literacy* guide, locating your state alliance, and obtaining a world of on-line geography education materials appears below. If you have any questions, the Society and the state alliances it supports are great places to start.

Whether you are an experienced geo-educator or a newcomer, the Bee is a sure bet to stir student interest in this "Why of Where" subject. Running the contest is simple. The Society provides a procedure booklet, the questions and answers, and accompanying overheads, certificates, and prizes. Think of the Bee as an open door to a world of fun and productive learning at a time when we all need to know more about "the world and all that is in it."

GEOGRAPHIC SUPPORT COORDINATES
To register for the National Geographic Bee
Principals of eligible U.S. schools can write to

National Geographic Bee
National Geographic Society
1145 17th Street N.W.
Washington, D.C. 20036-4688

Principals of U.S. schools with students in grades four through eight must register their schools to participate in the National Geographic Bee before the October 15 deadline. Principals may *request registration by writing on school letterhead and enclosing a check for $50 (U.S. funds; cost in 2004) made payable to the National Geographic Society. Call 202-828-6659 or go to www.nationalgeographic.com/geographicbee for the most current information.*

To register for the Canadian GeoChallenge
Canadian residents call 1-888-201-5022

To find your state geographic alliance office
www.nationalgeographic.com/education/teacher_community/

To order *Path Toward World Literacy*
Contact your state geographic alliance or write to
    The Grosvenor Center for Geographic Education
    Southwest Texas State University
    601 University Drive
    San Marcos, Texas 98666

To contact the National Geographic Education Foundation
www.nationalgeographic.com/foundation/

8. Israel
9. Turkey
10. Philippines

Round 7
3. Tanzania
4. Kurds
5. Buenos Aires
6. Cyprus
7. Lesser Antilles
8. Poland
9. Brunei
10. Greece

Tiebreaker Questions
2. Minsk
3. Argentina
4. Morocco
5. aqueduct
6. Sierra Madre Occidental

Immigration Graph
2. 1930s and 1940s
3. South America
4. 1960s
5. Africa, North America
6. Asia
7. North America

Photo Questions
2. Greece
3. salt

4. Matterhorn

Map Questions
2. 22, Zimbabwe
3. 24, Madagascar
4. 3, Tunisia

NATIONAL LEVEL
Round 1
1. Arabian
2. Estonia
3. Belize

Round 2
1. Australia
2. Mozambique
3. Kazakhstan

Round 3
1. Africa
2. China
3. Buddhism

Round 4
1. Beijing, Taipei, Manila
2. Volga, Danube, Elbe
3. Cameroon

Round 5
1. moraine
2. Köppen
3. guyot

Map Questions
13. 2
14. 3

STATE-LEVEL
Round 1
3. Mexico
4. Netherlands
5. Italy
6. Jerusalem
7. India
8. Russia
9. Cairo
10. Kalahari

Round 2
3. topographic map
4. evergreen tree
5. Antarctic Circle
6. igneous
7. front
8. marine west coast climate
9. fault
10. biosphere

Round 3
3. El Salvador
4. Atlas Mountains
5. Russia
6. China
7. Bolivia
8. Paris

9. Vatican City
10. Europe

Round 4
3. Poland
4. tourism
5. North Sea
6. Suez Canal
7. Arabian Peninsula
8. diamonds
9. Japan
10. Ethiopia

Round 5
1. Yemen
2. France
3. Korea, or Korean
4. Yugoslavia
5. Denmark
6. Eritrea
7. El Salvador
8. London
9. Norway
10. Uganda

Round 6
3. Nigeria
4. Siberia
5. Angola, Mozambique
6. Nuremberg
7. Cuba

One of the world's largest nonprofit scientific and educational organizations, the National Geographic Society was founded in 1888 "for the increase and diffusion of geographic knowledge." Fulfilling this mission, the Society educates and inspires millions every day through its magazines, books, television programs, videos, maps and atlases, research grants, the National Geographic Bee, teacher workshops, and innovative classroom materials. The Society is supported through membership dues, charitable gifts, and income from the sale of its educational products. This support is vital to National Geographic's mission to increase global understanding and promote conservation of our planet through exploration, research, and education.

For more information, please call 1-800-NGS LINE (647-5463)
or write to the following address:

National Geographic Society
1145 17th Street N.W.
Washington, D.C. 20036-4688 U.S.A.
Visit the Society's Web site: www.nationalgeographic.com

About the Author

Stephen F. Cunha is a professor of geography at California's Humboldt State University. He is also director of the California Geographic Alliance and state coordinator for the National Geographic Bee. Cunha has also worked for ten seasons as a national park ranger in Alaska and California. He and his family now live near Redwood National Park.

Acknowledgments

Many talented people contributed to this book. Thanking Mary Hackett of the California Geographic Alliance for Russian around on our behalf requires a book in itself. I would have Ghana crazy without Mary Lee Elden, Karen Blank, and Chelsea Zillmer of the National Geographic Bee staff, who provided the questions. Judy Walton, Professor of Geography at Humboldt State University, gave the resource chapter a good Czech. I would have Benin the dark about the Great Canadian Geography Challenge without Dale Gregory of Centennial School, British Columbia. The Bee kids who are the Seoul of Chapter 5 were totally cool. Most important, I Congo on and on about Suzanne Patrick Fonda of National Geographic Children's Books, but Midway through the writing it became evident that Oman, without her input, this volume would've met a Chile reception. Now that we are Finnish, I hope it makes you Hungary to learn Samoa geography!

Credits

Quotes from Bee winners on the back cover are from "Reflections on the National Geography Bee: State Champions Remember," by Christian H. Brill (1992, 1992 Arkansas State Finalist), University of Virginia, 1999; p.7, Brian Andreas's quote appears in *Geography,* by StoryPeople (www.storypeople.com); p. 11, Muhammad Ahmad Faris's quote appears in *The Home Planet,* conceived and edited by Kevin W. Kelly for the Association of Space Explorers, Addison-Wesley Publishing Company, New York, and Mir Publishers, Moscow; art p. 36, Shusei Nagaoka; p. 92 (both), Gordon Gahan; p. 93 upper, Volkmar Wentzel; p. 93 lower, Thomas J. Abercrombie; front cover, Mark Thiessen, NGP; back cover top and center left, Mark Thiessen, NGP; right and bottom left, Maria Stenzel.